ABOUT THE AUTHORS

JAMES ALTUCHER is an entrepreneur, investor, writer, and media personality who is known for, among other business endeavors, starting Stock-pickr.com, a "MySpace for Finance" that was quickly adopted by millions of users and was sold to TheStreet .com in 2007. Altucher contributes regularly to *The Wall Street Journal*, AOL Finance, the *Financial Times*, TheStreet.com, Yahoo Finance, the *Huffington Post*, and other media outlets. He also appears regularly on CNBC, Fox News, Fox Business, and CNN Radio. He is the author of four books: *Trade Like a Hedge Fund*, *Trade Like Warren Buffett*, *SuperCash*, and *The Forever Portfolio*.

DOUGLAS R. SEASE is a writer and editor. He was a reporter and editor for *The Wall Street Journal* for twenty-six years, covering or supervising coverage of steel, autos, international trade, and finance. His team of reporters was nominated for a Pulitzer Prize in 1993 for extensive coverage of the problems caused by financial derivatives long before they became the underlying cause of the Great Financial Crisis of 2008. Mr. Sease is the author of five books on investing and tax policy and has edited or ghostwritten more than a dozen books on management, finance, government, and foreign business.

THE WALL STREET JOURNAL GUIDE TO

Investing in the Apocalypse

THE WALL STREET JOURNAL GUIDE TO

Investing in the Apocalypse

Make Money by Seeing Opportunity

Where Others See Peril

JAMES ALTUCHER

and

DOUGLAS R. SEASE

HARPER
BUSINESS

HARPER
BUSINESS

THE WALL STREET JOURNAL GUIDE TO INVESTING IN THE APOCALYPSE. Copyright © 2011 by Dow Jones and Company. All rights reserved. Printed in the United States of America. No part of this book may be used or reproduced in any manner whatsoever without written permission except in the case of brief quotations embodied in critical articles and reviews. For information address HarperCollins Publishers, 10 East 53rd Street, New York, NY 10022.

HarperCollins books may be purchased for educational, business, or sales promotional use. For information please write: Special Markets Department, HarperCollins Publishers, 10 East 53rd Street, New York, NY 10022.

FIRST EDITION

Library of Congress Cataloging-in-Publication Data is available upon request.

ISBN 978-0-06-200132-0

11 12 13 14 15 OV/RRD 10 9 8 7 6 5 4 3 2 1

For Claudia Altucher, I hope you survive me if any of these apocalyptic chapters come true.

For Jane Sease, my partner and best friend in good times and bad.

CONTENTS

THE WALL STREET JOURNAL GUIDE TO

Investing in the Apocalypse

HOW WILL THE WORLD as we know it end? Will it be with a whimper as the last human beings succumb to some viral epidemic sweeping the globe? Or will it be with a bang when an asteroid slams into the planet? No one knows for sure. But what we do know is that there will be some very close calls that will be scary. A pandemic spreads. A terrorist detonates a nuclear bomb in a major city and claims to have more ready to explode. Ice caps melt, coastlines are submerged, and crops wither from drought. Clean fresh water becomes increasingly difficult to obtain. Or maybe it is oil that becomes scarce. Or a global financial panic erupts that regulators cannot contain. Any one of those scenarios could occur in our lifetimes. The one thing they all have in common is that their occurrence will touch off panic and, in some cases, hysteria. As a result, these events will also contain the seeds of profit for investors who stay calm and think rather than panic and run.

That said, one important note before we go any further: while this book deals with some truly frightening events—some of which will almost certainly happen one day—we aren't setting out to worsen your fears. Rather we want to show you, first, how you can overcome those fears by putting many of these events in their proper perspective. Then, we want to explain how to prepare your finances not just to survive an event should it strike, but to prosper as a result. We don't want people to get sick; we don't want another terrorist attack; and we certainly hope the planet doesn't cook itself into oblivion. However, there are people out there thinking about these things very hard and trying to find solutions. Many of those who succeed will become justly wealthy and there's no reason you shouldn't take advantage of their good fortune and make it part of yours. In *The Wall Street Journal Guide to Investing in the Apocalypse* we want to help you think about these unthinkable events, defend your financial life against their consequences, and maybe even emerge in better shape than before they happened.

What This Book Is About

At the heart of this book lies our observation that historically significant events—the assassination of a president or an archduke, an economic depression, or a global pandemic—have a significant, and observable, impact on investments. We believe that, in the face of apparent cataclysm, the professional traders and money managers, along with hordes of ordinary investors, will lose their nerve and desperately seek the safety of cash or even gold. The mad rush to sell will drive the prices of a broad array of securities and other assets far below any concept of fair value. Prices will reflect the investors' assumption of the worst.

But what if the worst doesn't occur? In that case all but the most shaken eventually will return to the financial and other markets. Their purchases will then drive asset prices higher, perhaps back to fair value or beyond. In any event, those who did not assume the worst and bought the assets all the others were selling will stand to profit handsomely as prices rebound. This is contrarian investing in the most basic sense. The opportunities don't come along often, but when they do they can make a huge difference in investment performance for those with a steady hand, an analytic mind, and an optimistic outlook. We call this methodology "event-based investing," and this book is a guide to mastering it.

What constitutes an event? In this book, we'll use that term to refer to anything that threatens to upset the normal ebb and flow of markets and economies. Most people think of an event as something that occurs suddenly, such as the explosion of a terrorist bomb or a political assassination. But events can occur over much longer periods of time, ranging from days to years to decades. The Great Depression that plunged the United States into despair was an event, as was World War II, which saved the world from tyranny and reignited our nation's economy at the same time. Viruses that cause pandemics may hover threateningly in the background for years before suddenly blossoming and doing their worst damage. Global warming scenarios will play out over decades.

Also, different events inspire different levels of fear. Terrorism touches off immediate fear, a pandemic creates gradually escalating levels of fear over a period of months and, at least for the moment, few people appear to be even the least bit worried about the looming global shortage of fresh water. How fast or slow an event occurs and what degree of fear it inspires doesn't change the possibility of defending against it and perhaps profiting from it, only the time it takes to make a decision and act on it.

Event-based investing is not for everyone. It requires an ability to anticipate seemingly earth-shattering events and to measure the risks appropriately. It also insists that you think unemotionally about the consequences of both the anticipated event occurring and of the possibility that it won't occur or that the consequences will not be as fearsome as others predict. In *The Wall Street Journal Guide to Investing in the Apocalypse* we purposely push the concept of event-based investing to the farthest edges of what might be possible. In the coming pages we will closely analyze several potential global threats, the probabilities of their occurring, and the opportunities they might present for the contrarian investor who doesn't fall victim to hype and hysteria. Some of these events will be man-made: financial catastrophe, for example, stems from human actions. Others, such as pandemics, are rooted in nature. Some of the events we discuss are related: global warming and the coming shortage of clean fresh water have common roots in the burgeoning world population. And some are more likely to occur than others. The challenge for investors is how to get ahead of the curve now to reap profits in 2020 or beyond.

While we admit to pushing the envelope in our analysis of potentially apocalyptic events, we firmly believe that the lessons and disciplines that we draw from these chapters are useful for much more likely and much less catastrophic events. No portfolio should be based solely on playing the angles of the day's news. Long-term investing with a widely diversified portfolio has been and will remain the core of a successful approach to investing for almost all individuals (and, truth be told, for professionals, too). Nevertheless, an understanding of how to think about the implications of events much less awe-inspiring than the apocalypse can provide a significant performance advantage for investors alert to the possibilities.

Event-based investing need not—indeed, should not—be complicated. There is little new under the investing sun and some of those things that are new—collateralized debt obligations and other exotic financial derivatives—almost spelled our doom in 2008. Our approach to apocalyptic investing can be done straightforwardly with simple securities that are easy to understand, such as stocks, bonds, and even mutual funds. Those with a bent for investing may enhance their returns through the use of options. The difference between this and other investing books is that we offer a way to think about investing that, while using simple tools, provides a sophisticated strategic approach that can become an integral part of a broader long-term portfolio of diversified assets.

It is always risky to name stocks in a book intended to serve investors for years, but we take that risk for two reasons. First, there are some companies that should be in any long-term portfolio because of their potential to soar in times of crisis. These are companies that are engaged in worthy and profitable endeavors that will be able to bring expertise and financial muscle to solving the problems that threaten us. Second, we will highlight some companies because they demonstrate how to execute an event-based investment strategy assuming certain conditions. In other words, these companies illustrate our approach, but shouldn't necessarily become part of your portfolio of apocalyptic investments. And in the interest of full disclosure, you need to know that Douglas Sease owns shares of General Electric in a long-term retirement account and that, at the time of publication, James Altucher, or any entity managed by James Altucher, owns none of the stocks mentioned in this book. In the end this book is intended to help investors learn to think about finding the companies and other assets, both large and small, that will be the beneficiaries of various cataclysms.

What This Book Is Not About

A note of caution: many investors approaching the subject of apocalyptic investing will assume right away that the best way to play an impending cataclysm is by shorting relevant stocks. Sorry to disappoint you, but we do not advocate any short selling as part of event-based investing. We believe short selling is one of the most dangerous tactics that can be undertaken by investors, and that belief is based on both logic and experience: We have seen too many seemingly knowledgeable traders and investors wiped out by trying to profit from decline.

Despite our title, this book also isn't about gloom and doom. Quite the contrary. It is about hope and optimism and the fruits of innovation. Consider that two of the great sources of both human misery and human progress have been war and disease. Technologies created or improved by the military working with private enterprise—jet engines, satellites, and the Internet, for example—have given us the benefit of global travel, an unprecedented ability to communicate with one another, and easy access to unimaginable amounts of information. The quest to overcome disease has given us longer life spans, better health, and incredible gains in human productivity. Many people despaired at the prospect of war or epidemics, but others took up the challenges and created products and processes that preserved democracy and lives. We fully expect to be chastised by some for seeking profits in disaster, but we believe that one of the preeminent messages of capitalism is, "We solve problems."

How to Use This Book

While we intend this volume to be instructive and informative, we also want it to be a compelling read. Many of the potential events we use to teach the lessons of *Investing in the Apocalypse* involve scientific complexity. We will use anecdotes and illustrations and a well-honed ability to present complex subjects in layman's language to make clear what is at the root of each potential calamity. Where controversy exists, we will present both sides of the argument while nevertheless taking the side that we believe makes the most sense. But one of the major lessons we teach in this book is that it isn't simply what you think or know that creates an investment opportunity, it is what the vast majority thinks or thinks they know. Understanding mass perceptions of events is crucial to finding opportunity where others see hazard.

The first chapter presents basic information about the history of cataclysms and markets and the fundamentals of investing that form the foundation for our analysis of specific threats to civilization. The history of the human race has seen countless disasters, including the Black Death and many other pandemics; untold numbers of wars and genocides that took hundreds of millions of lives; and devastating earthquakes, tsunamis, floods, and droughts. Yet human ingenuity and ambition have overcome them all, and the human race continues to progress and prosper.

After that beginning we introduce each of the specific threats, one chapter at a time. After explaining what is known and what is debatable in each threat we move to the investment opportunities. We acknowledge that some investors are more conservative than others. The more conservative you are, the smaller the portion of your overall portfolio should be devoted to apocalyptic themes. We will, where feasible, suggest company names as long-term plays—GlaxoSmithKline, for instance, is a solid long-term bet to profit from pandemics—or for illustrative purposes. But for the most part the companies we name will be representative of the kinds of stocks one should examine, such as manufacturers of various energy-efficient products that contribute to the effort to slow perceived global warming. And while we do not advocate short selling, we will point out areas to avoid, such as the airlines and big-box retailers that would suffer in the event of a large-scale pandemic that prompts people to avoid direct contact with others.

We hope you find *Investing in the Apocalypse* illuminating rather than frightening, optimistic rather than pessimistic, and, ultimately, both useful and entertaining.

ONE

AN ILL WIND

The Fundamentals of Apocalyptic Investing

I T WAS A BEAUTIFUL fall day in Dallas. Men, women, and children were gathered on the plaza to watch the president's motorcade pass. As the big Cadillac convertible wheeled through Dealey Plaza and turned onto Elm Street, John F. Kennedy flashed his emblematic grin and raised his right hand to wave. As he did the *pop, pop, pop* of gunfire rang out. Kennedy clutched his fists around his head and neck and rolled to his left, shot through the back by the first bullet. The second bullet struck his head, delivering the fatal blow. The world's most vibrant and powerful leader, the man who had faced down the Soviet Union in Cuba, whose attractive and elegant family had turned Washington into Camelot during his brief tenure, was dead.

The entire world was stunned. The Cold War was still raging

and some thought the assassination might touch off a global nuclear war. But mostly the reaction was one of a shared tragedy. People wept openly in public. Traffic came to a standstill as people tuned in to news broadcasts. Schools were closed, businesses shut early. Even those people who were only seven or eight years old at the time—and barely old enough to be cognizant of the event—still remember what they were doing when they heard the news.

The news of Kennedy's death hit the floor of the New York Stock Exchange within minutes of the event. The uncertainty of what lay ahead for the nation in the wake of the assassination sent the Dow Jones Industrial Average down 3% that day—a "minicrash" but still a remarkable drop given the lack of volatility in the stock market in the early 1960s. Yet two trading days later, with a new president sworn in and the alleged assassin captured, the market regained the losses that resulted from Kennedy's death and a five-year bull market began. Optimism had yet again won the day.

We are at heart a nation of optimists, although you wouldn't know that by talking to people, reading the newspapers or blogs, or watching much that appears on television. In the media it's gloom and doom 24/7, and most people would rather complain than compliment. Yet a brief tour through American history over the past century with a focus on some of most disturbing events reveals a markedly different story told through the stock market, one of the best barometers for our collective sense of the future. It is the story of resilience in the face of disaster.

CRISIS AND THE FINANCIAL MARKETS: A BRIEF HISTORY

THE GREAT DEPRESSION AND WORLD WAR II

The worst economic crisis that the United States has faced was the Great Depression. We all know the scenes of misery: the poverty-stricken farm woman clutching her child clad in rags, the camps of migrant farmers, and the bread lines and soup kitchens. Millions were unemployed for years, and millions more lost their life savings. Then came World War II and the massive effort to save the world from Nazi domination. The war itself corrected the unemployment problem and jump-started moribund industries, including steel, autos (which turned its factories to making tanks and bombers), shipbuilding, and chemicals. The Dow Jones Industrial Average, which had hit a low of 41.22 in 1932, ended World War II at 191.98. Two of what might have been the ultimate disasters—economic depression and war—in reality set the stage for unbelievable opportunities.

THE THREAT OF NUCLEAR WAR

Even as economic growth swelled in the 1950s a new specter arose: the threat of globally devastating nuclear war with the Soviet Union. And we came frighteningly close to suffering the consequences in the fall of 1962 when U.S. spy planes discovered Russian missiles in Cuba. The Cuban Missile Crisis and the prospect of nuclear incineration sent the Standard & Poor's 500 Index plunging. Yet less than a month after the announcement of the missiles the S&P was in record territory.

THE ARAB OIL EMBARGO

Much of our economic growth after World War II was fueled by cheap oil. But in 1973 the nations that exported all that oil decided to push for much higher prices and ultimately embargoed shipments of oil to the United States, touching off panic among people who were accustomed to filling their gas tanks with twenty-cents-a-gallon gasoline. Coupled with the breakout of war in the Middle East, a severe recession triggered by raging inflation, and the scandal of a U.S. president caught in criminal conduct, this oil crisis dealt our spirits a hard blow and stock prices reflected it. In January 1973, the Dow Jones Industrial Average reached a high of 1067 before plunging over the next two years to a low of 570 in December 1974, not to regain its former glory until 1982. This lost decade was similar to what we are experiencing now.

THE SOUTH AMERICAN DEBT CRISIS

In 1982 our largest trading partners were Mexico and some of the larger countries in South America. The eight largest U.S. banks had loaned 260% of their capital to those countries, more than is currently on loan to Europe. Then in rough order Mexico, Brazil, Argentina, Chile, and several other South American countries defaulted on their debts. They didn't just threaten to default to gain leverage with the banks; they actually failed to pay notes when due. Coming as they did on the heels of the worst U.S. recession since World War II, those defaults threatened to undermine the global economy. But the U.S. government formulated a plan to bail out those countries through a restructuring of their debts, and the plan worked. The stock market rose an astounding 49% in 1982 and 1983.

THE 1987 MARKET CRASH

Banks and government officials had realized that Mexico, Brazil, and Argentina were headed for trouble long before the defaults occurred and so were at least psychologically prepared for problems. But on October 19, 1987, no one was prepared for the Dow

Jones Industrial Average to plunge 27% in a single day amid a cascade of computer-generated selling. But we did have a brief warning that trouble was looming. On October 14 stocks fell a record-breaking 95.46 points and then another 58 points the next day. On Friday, October 16, the London stock market was closed because of a lashing North Atlantic storm and the Dow set another record for a one-day drop, 108.35 points on record volume. This rapid decline left investors with a weekend in which to ponder their much-reduced portfolios.

The real trouble began the following Monday morning in Hong Kong, where prices plummeted 45%. In an already gloomy mood, investors in other countries sold heavily, too. When trading began in New York the wave of selling was overwhelming. The decline still stands as the single largest percentage drop in U.S. market history, and, at the time, it seemed like the end of the financial world as we knew it. Today, however, we look back on Black Monday as some kind of weird anomaly for which there are lots of explanations, none particularly convincing. The market bottomed on October 20 and wound up recovering all of its losses and closing the year at 1,939 points, a gain of 2.2%.

THE ASIAN FINANCIAL CRISIS OF 1997

Next up was the Asian Financial Crisis in 1997 that touched off fears of a global financial meltdown. The crisis began in Thailand when the Thai government bowed to continued pressure on its currency, the baht, and cut it loose from its ties to the U.S. dollar. The baht plunged as global investors who had speculated on the currency realized that Thailand's foreign debts essentially meant the country was insolvent. The crisis rapidly spread to other Asian countries, especially in Southeast Asia. Even Japan was affected. The financial contagion eventually swept across the ocean and, on October 27, 1997, took the Dow Jones Industrial Average down

7%. But the United States–backed International Monetary Fund bailed out Asia, interest rates were cut to stimulate growth, and the Dow ended 1997 higher than it began. Asian markets recovered fully a few years later.

9/11

Although there were other events that seemed to hold the potential to be devastating, the climactic crisis came on September 11, 2001, when a small band of determined terrorists flew hijacked passenger planes into both towers of the World Trade Center and the Pentagon, as well as into a field in Pennsylvania. The collapse of the towers, situated so near the New York Stock Exchange in lower Manhattan, shut down trading for five days. A nation already beset by the bursting of the dot-com bubble, a recession, and widespread corporate corruption epitomized by the collapse of Enron reeled under the blow of the 9/11 attacks. After trading was restored on September 17 the S&P 500 tumbled from its September 10 level of 1,092 to 944.75. Yet six months later the S&P was at 1,165.55, well above that preattack level.

THE GREAT RECESSION OF 2008–9

This was perhaps the closest call the world has ever had to financial collapse. It was a classic example of a speculative bubble bursting. Like most bubbles the stage was set when almost everyone believed that real estate prices could move in only one direction—straight up. There is certainly plenty of blame to pass around: unscrupulous mortgage brokers shoving money at willing or unwitting borrowers eager to cash in on the real estate boom; bankers and investment firms creating ever more complex financial instruments to sell to one another with no understanding of how those instruments might behave in a panic; but never mind pointing fingers. The point was an investor who saw the bubble reaching titanic proportions in 2007 could have gotten out of the markets for both real estate and stocks—the two most overblown in terms of unrealistic prices—and waited for the popping sound that signaled the end of the good times, at least for those who stayed in those markets. That's the classic smart way to play a bubble. The trouble was this bubble was so big that it nearly took down the global financial system.

Today we seem to have averted the collapse of the financial system. But the effects of the bursting bubble and the deep recession it caused will likely be with us for years to come. Unemployment looks to be an intractable problem and real estate prices probably have farther to fall to clear the market of all those foreclosed and abandoned houses and condos. Yet for that savvy investor who left the markets in 2007, the crisis atmosphere that pervaded the financial world in 2008 presented some wonderful opportunities in the form of hundreds, if not thousands, of stocks trading at unprecedented low prices. If the money that came out of the stock market in 2007 had gone back in during the worst of the crisis in 2008, an investor would have scored in a big way.

We admit that investing in events like those we just discussed sounds frightening. But you might not have picked up the book if we had called it what it really is: opportunistic investing. While we do present scenarios in the remainder of the book that are indeed frightening and suggest ways to take advantage of them, we are using those situations to illustrate and teach a broader lesson: markets are not rational and they will occasionally provide you the opportunity to profit from others' irrationality. The key is knowing how to recognize opportunity when it comes calling and seize the moment. And it's simpler than you think. If you're thinking you need to be a trading genius with multiple computer screens and several different brokerage accounts to invest in the apocalypse you've got it all wrong. Anyone with a moderate interest in markets and personal finance can take advantage of the approach we advocate. And just to prove our point, let us tell you about our own methodologies for investing, with a particular focus on opportunistic investing. They couldn't be more different from each other.

Doug's Approach

Since writing *The Wall Street Journal*'s daily stock market column in the late 1980s and then overseeing the paper's markets coverage for much of the 1990s, I long ago concluded that the KISS (Keep It Simple, Stupid) approach to investing best suits my temperament and interest in investing. Over the course of my market coverage I interviewed hundreds of money managers and found that while most of them are smart and seemed to be able to build a logical argument for whatever their advice was, they often got it wrong. Fortunately, because they wanted to be mentioned in the paper I got most of that (bad) advice free. Also fortunately, because of the paper's strict conflict of interest rules, I couldn't have acted on it anyway. But it certainly caused me to wonder what all those people with brokerage and advisory accounts were getting for the fees they paid.

I took a different path. I concentrate most of my investments in low-cost index funds and no-cost Treasury bonds.

That doesn't mean that I have a simple portfolio, particularly if you consider my desire for diversification. I own funds that invest in big stocks, as well as those that invest in mid caps and small caps. I have a low-cost junk bond fund and I own several international index funds that focus variously on Europe, Asia, emerging markets, and international small-cap stocks. I stash cash in a money market fund and in a short-term bond index fund and I've gradually been building a bond ladder comprised of ten-year inflation-protected treasuries in my largest retirement account. All told, through my funds I own thousands of stocks around the world, yet I can keep track of all that with a simple one-page spreadsheet that I update once a month. No calls to or from brokers, no complicated paperwork at tax time, and no time spent studying annual reports and other information looking (often fruitlessly) for the trigger point to buy or sell a particular stock.

That isn't to say that my approach is "Buy it and forget it," or that I don't stay alert to opportunity. But the opportunity has to be big to make it worth the effort. The recent Great Financial Crisis was exactly that kind of opportunity. From my perspective in Florida, the real estate boom that engulfed much of the nation in the early part of the new century began to look awfully dangerous. Condos and houses were flipping from one buyer to the next often before they were even built. Prices were climbing at unimaginable speed and land was being cleared rapidly for new developments. Real estate salespeople were regularly calling to ask me if I wanted to sell or knew someone who did so they could get the listing.

As the real estate market soared in the early 2000s, I knew that much of it was being driven by the use of derivatives. The more frantic it all became, the more I concluded it wasn't going to end well, either for real estate or the economy and markets in general. In 2007 I began systematically reducing my overall exposure to stocks. Of course, we never get the timing right and I was feeling a little foolish sitting on a stash of cash in a money market account as the market kept rising. Still, I steadily pulled money out. Then came Bear Stearns's brush with death followed by Lehman Brothers' collapse, and the rest is history still being made.

As global markets reeled and banks and brokerages teetered on the edge of collapse, I decided to take a big risk. Once again I was a little off on the timing, putting cash back into the market even as it fell. I certainly can't claim I felt any confidence that the government that had caused the problem had any great fixes for the financial crisis, but I also didn't think the utter collapse of capitalism was upon us. I could have been wrong, in which case I would be looking today at a catastrophically reduced investment portfolio. But I wasn't. Eventually the markets hit bottom and the rebound began. My decision to partially leave, then return to the markets is a classic example of apocalyptic investing. First it was the rising bubble that seemed—and was—too good to be true. Then just the opposite: the sky was falling, panic was everywhere, and values were being driven to what seemed to be ridiculously low levels. Taking the chance seemed worth the risk given the potential long-term gains.

Obviously given my approach to investing I don't get many opportunities to make bold moves like I did in 2007 and again in 2008. But that's fine with me. I don't need a lot of excitement in my investing portfolio.

James's Approach

Doug is a writer, not a professional investor. For that reason his approach to investing and the way he thinks about apocalyptic events is fine. It suits his style and interests. I, on the other hand, for the past fifteen years have been professionally involved with many different styles of investing: futures trading, day trading, value investing, arbitrage, and private equity investing, to name a few. I have also invested in private businesses as a venture capitalist, been an entrepreneur who has successfully started and sold three different businesses, run a fund of hedge funds, and day-traded for proprietary trading firms. I've bought and sold millions of shares of stocks, futures, debt deals, and venture deals, among other instruments. And as an entrepreneur I've learned to try to anticipate every possible scenario that could block me from making the month's payroll, because if the payroll wasn't paid out of my revenue, it was paid out of my pocket. I know all the stuff about great investors being self-confident and bold, but I've got to tell you that the pervasive theme running through my career as a professional investor has been worry.

To some extent I regret every minute of these past fifteen years. People always say, "Oh, I have no regrets." Liars! Investing is no fun at all. My brain is scarred from the nonstop worry. Being a good investor—not great, just good—requires you to attempt to anticipate every event you can possibly imagine, from the most extreme at a global level, such as nuclear war, to the most minute details of the investment itself: Is the company or hedge fund I'm investing in run by good people? Is it a fraud? How are cash flows this year? When day-trading there's an additional factor to consider, and that's your own physiology and how that affects your psychology. Are you getting enough sleep? Did you have a fight with your girlfriend and now you're going to take it out on the market? Are you eating well and staying in shape? Everything counts in investing and over the past fifteen years I've seen every way in which this market is rigged, manipulated, and scammed. But ultimately, good companies win and the companies that are innovative and can anticipate world-changing events will do especially well. And if a company isn't innovating, by definition it is dying.

I could be considered a dilettante of investing. I prefer to think of myself as a student, always curious about new, and hopefully better, ways to make money and serve my clients. With the media constantly obsessing every day on the "new new thing" that could cause the world's end, I started studying the ways in which investors could construct their portfolios to anticipate cataclysmic events before they occur. Combined with a trading approach that will work when the actual events or crises happen, this will generate solid returns during the trials ahead of us.

This book is the combination of the various philosophies

I've used to trade successfully over the years. It is a trading approach that combines hard-core fundamentals and both micro- and macroanalysis. The driving force, though, behind every style of investing is an ability to worry combined with the ability to rationally focus that worry into decisions that will either make money or help you avoid losing money. It helps to remember Warren Buffett's two most important rules of investing: First, don't lose money; second, don't forget rule number one.

Some Investment Basics

Whether you're a mostly passive investor like Doug or more active like James, there are nevertheless some fundamental points we think you need to keep in mind when investing, whether in routine markets or during apocalyptic crises. You probably already know these fundamentals, but it's worth reviewing them quickly before we move into a more detailed explanation of investing in the apocalypse.

Diversification is important. You will almost always have the best opportunities for making big profits in stocks. That's why you will find us suggesting mostly stocks as the vehicles to seize the opportunities presented by the various apocalyptic scenarios we outline. In any given year there is one stock out of the many thousands traded that outperforms all the others. If you own that stock you will do very, very well. But there is also one stock out of them all that performs the worst. Own that one and you will be crying in your beer. That's why you should always own a portfolio of stocks, not just one. If one plunges, chances are that the others won't.

While stocks offer the best potential for profit, they also offer the most risk. Reward does not come without risk. And there are times—2008 was one of them—when almost all stocks fall and fall sharply. Bonds, money market funds, and other "safe havens" are safe precisely because they provide less risk as well as less reward. They serve to temper the volatility of stocks and you shouldn't kid yourself: volatility can hurt, both financially and psychologically. We know many investors who before the heavy sell-off of 2008 were convinced they could weather a storm of selling, but who were so frightened by the magnitude of the market's decline that they did the worst thing possible and gave in to their fears as the market approached its bottom. They remained so shaken that they missed most of the big gains that occurred in 2009 and 2010 as the market recovered its equilibrium. The more money you have in safe havens, the less likely you'll be tempted to sell when the storm occurs. It's also true that the more money you have in safe havens the more ammunition you will have to take advantage of a sudden apocalyptic event and the opportunity it presents. It's a balancing game between safety and potential gains or losses, and only you can know where you stand on that particular balance beam.

Goals govern everything. How you invest and what you invest in depend upon the goals underlying your investment program. If you will need a substantial amount of cash in the next few years to buy a second home, send the kids to college, or undertake any other large expenditure, the money for that should not be in stocks. There's simply too much risk that the market will be down when you need the money and you'll be forced to lock in a loss. But if it's retirement you're thinking about funding, then stocks are your game. We don't adhere to the usual advice that as you grow older you shift a big portion of your portfolio into bonds. Bonds have their place, but someone sixty years old today with a reasonable nest egg should have 75% or more of a retirement portfolio invested in stocks, consistent with his or her risk tolerance. After all, life expectancy for someone who is now sixty is twenty more years. There's a lot of money to be made in stocks over that period of time. More to the point of this book, there are apocalyptic scenarios that will play out quickly, in a matter of hours, days, or months, and there are scenarios that will play out over the lifetime of our children and grandchildren. Investing money that you intend to go to young heirs years from now in one or more of those long-term scenarios will be doing them a huge favor.

Management matters. Since stocks are the vehicles we overwhelmingly favor for investing in the apocalypse, we think you need to know something about both the management and the finances of a company you're considering buying. There will always be multiple companies that may profit from the consequences of an apocalyptic event, but some will be better managed and better financed than others. All other things being equal, it's your job to do the research and make that call in favor of the better managed and financed company for your investment.

Stuff happens. That's why stocks are risky. But when it hits the fan, it can be either good or bad, depending on your position in a stock. Let's take a well-known example, Transocean, the company that builds and leases deepwater drilling equipment around the world. At the beginning of 2010 Transocean (RIG) was trading at nearly $95 a share. Without taking into account whether that was a good value at the moment, it would logically be a candidate for inclusion in a portfolio aimed at benefitting from the apocalyptic scenario of "peak oil," the situation that occurs when the world is using more oil than is being produced. We know lots of oil exists in reservoirs under the ocean, but it's very difficult to extract and Transocean was on the cutting edge of deepwater drilling. Then, of course, the company's Deepwater Horizon semisubmersible platform in the Gulf of Mexico blew up, sank, and started a gusher of oil flowing into the Gulf nearly a mile below the surface. At the height of the crisis Transocean's stock price fell to $41.88. If you had bought it in January 2010, your investment, like the oil leak, would be deep underwater. But if you didn't own it, the tragic accident may have presented you with a great opportunity. It all depends on your view of how likely the world is to keep exploring for oil in deep water.

Short selling is a short path to financial ruin. Short selling occurs when an investor borrows a stock and sells it in the expectation that he can buy it later at a lower price and return it to the lender, nailing a profit in the process. It's a tempting strategy for investing in the apocalypse. Say a global flu pandemic begins to spread, millions of people are sick, and everyone else is terrified of catching the virus. Wouldn't it make sense to short the stocks of retailers, movie chains, restaurants, and any other place that consumers would shun for fear of getting sick?

Sorry, no. As we mentioned in the introduction, it certainly sounds good, but history shows us that short selling is a loser's strategy. Only in rare circumstances do short sellers make money. Take 2001, for example, one of the worst years in market history. The 9/11 attacks occurred; Enron, Tyco, and WorldCom exposed deep ethical flaws in corporate America; and the Nasdaq fell more than 20% as the dot-com bubble burst. A great year for shorting, wouldn't you think? Well, the CSFB Dedicated Shortsellers Index, comprised of hedge funds devoted to short selling—the Darth Vader of the stock market, in other words—fell 3% in a year it would have been logically expected to thrive. We've looked at various methodologies that promise big profits to short sellers and when examined in detail and over time, they just don't cut it. Better to simply stay away from a stock that's in trouble than short it.

There are three fundamental problems with short selling. First, the upside is limited. The best possible return on a short position is 100% and that occurs only if the stock you short goes to zero, a very rare event. But the downside of short selling is infinite. If a stock is selling for 5 and you short it at that price and the next day the company gets taken over by some conglomerate for $20 a share, you have just lost 400% of your money. In other words, you owe the bank money. The authors have known more than a few people who have gone personally bankrupt through the fine art of short selling. Finally the system is rigged against short sellers. We're currently passing through a period of deep malaise after one of incredible ebullience. Depending on how you measure it, stocks actually lost money over a ten-year period. But that is a rare occasion. Over the course of the past two hundred years, stocks have steadily gone higher and we presume that they will soon resume that trend. With that long-term drift upward, short sellers have never successfully made money over the long haul.

The Three Fundamental Principles of Apocalyptic Investing

With these investment basics in mind, we can now turn to apocalyptic investing, which actually isn't markedly different from any other kind of investing. You're still buying and selling stocks, calculating gains or losses, and paying taxes on your profits. What's different about it is that it requires a different way of *thinking* about investing. The fundamental principles are easy to state, but not always so easy to act upon. The chapters that follow, in which we detail some apocalyptic scenarios and suggest how to apply the three fundamental principles of apocalyptic investing, will do much to clarify how to think about investing.

Principle One: Fade the Fear

This principle is mostly aimed at getting you to think clearly and rationally while all around you people are terrified and acting irrationally. It assumes that what has been true in the past will be true in the future: no matter how bad things seem, they really aren't that bad. Eventually they will get better. We explained earlier, and we repeat here, that no one knows the future, and one day this principle may not work. An asteroid really may hit the earth and wipe out life as we know it. At that point your investment portfolio isn't going to matter at all. But until that cataclysmic event occurs and you and everyone else disappear in an earth-shattering blast, people will continue to imagine the worst and the worst will continue not to occur.

A primary example of fears that are not realized was the Great Financial Collapse of 2008. Many people, among them sophisticated financiers and nerveless professional traders, really did wonder if the end was nigh and acted on their fears, selling everything with no regard to valuations. What they didn't reckon with was the immense power of governments, both ours and others, to pull the financial system out of its downward spiral. But that is exactly what happened. You can argue all day about the cost of bailing out banks, whether the increase in deficit spending will curtail our future growth, or what might have happened had no governments intervened. But they did.

If you had the money and the courage to invest in late 2008 and early 2009, you're probably sitting on big profits. Even if you did nothing but sit still during the crisis you're still in pretty good shape. Granted, the value of your portfolio isn't what it was just prior to the collapse, but in one sense your portfolio really wasn't worth what your statement said it was. It reflected the massive bubble that had enveloped the world's economy. The crisis came when the bubble inevitably popped, and people reacted irrationally. We could argue that the market in mid-2010 represented a much more realistic valuation than did the pre-bubble highs, which were destined to fall when the bubble popped.

A less cataclysmic example of irrational fear dominating investors happened during the 2009 episode of pandemic flu caused by the H1N1 virus, which at the time was dubbed "swine flu." It was dubbed this after lab tests showed that the virus contained genes that are commonly found in influenza viruses that affect pigs in North America. But after further study it became evident that the virus causing the pandemic was more related to the viruses that usually affect birds and pigs in Europe and Asia. It was, in fact, a variant of bird flu. Nevertheless thousands of investors put in orders to sell stocks of any company remotely related to the pork industry. Smithfield Foods (SFD) is an example which fell severely that week. A stock that carried the unfortunate symbol HOGS fell 20%. (The actual company, Zhongpin, does in fact process pork.)

We discuss how to fade the fear in each of the examples of apocalyptic events that follow, but it is a valuable principle to apply to much more mundane situations. Typically if fear is present in palpable amounts in the stock market, prices of market indices will fall precipitously in the course of a single day's trading. We went back to 1955 to track what would happen had an investor simply bought the S&P 500 Index each time it fell 3% or more in one day. We found 84 days that met our criteria since 1955. In 48 cases, or 57% of the time, the market was higher a week later than it had been before the tumble. Averaged across all 84 incidents the market was higher by 0.67% a week after a 3% or more drop. That compares to the average weekly gain of the S&P 500 of 0.17%. So an investor who could "fade the fear" and buy when others were selling in panic could realize a gain four times greater than average.

Fading the fear works on individual stocks, too. We went back a decade to find individual stocks that fell at least 10% in a single day. A 10% decline in one day is a pretty sure indicator that people are fearful of owning the stock. There could be many reasons: a bad earnings report, a negative analyst report, legal actions, whatever. We found 4,177 times that a stock in the S&P 500 fell by at least 10% in a single day. Had an investor bought each of those stocks at the close of trading the day it fell, held a week, then sold it, he would have made money in 2,580 of those situations. What's more, the average gain across all such incidents a week would be 3.16%, for an annualized return of 160%.

Fear is your friend as long as you don't catch it.

Principle Two: Invest through the Back Door

This principle, as well as the third one, focuses more on how to think about specific investments in the context of a specific cataclysmic event. In other words, how to find the opportunities in a crisis. The first temptation that comes to mind if you can fade your fear and think clearheadedly about making money in a crisis is to focus on a specific company devoted in its entirety to solving the problem that caused the crisis. Is bird flu sweeping the globe? Buy the stock of the little Swiss genomics company working on the cure.

Wrong!

There are times and places to make speculative bets—and small companies betting on striking it rich with a single untested product are definitely speculative—but your first thought should be "capture some profits while covering my butt." To do that we recommend strongly that you consider what we call "back-door plays." These are companies that have a diverse product line, that generate steady cash flow in good times as well as bad, and that are not highly leveraged. You want a company that is interested in solving the problem causing the crisis but whose future doesn't depend solely on finding that sometimes elusive solution.

Almost by definition those companies will be larger than the speculative picks you might be tempted to make. Instead of the little genomics company we mentioned earlier you might want to consider GlaxoSmithKline (GLX), the huge pharmaceutical company that distributes most of the flu vaccines in the world. Consider three scenarios. If there really is a pandemic affecting much of the world's population, then GLX will make huge profits. If there is a fear of pandemic that doesn't materialize GLX will make large profits. And even if no pandemic arises, GLX will continue to make money at a fairly steady pace from an aging population and improved health care in developing countries. In and of itself, GLX is a good investment. It's an even better investment in the event of a pandemic. It's a back-door approach to profiting from disaster.

Principle Three: Invest through the Front Door

The back-door approach to investing is best used in situations in which a crisis may or may not develop suddenly and will end reasonably quickly, say within a few months or a year. The front-door approach is for longer-term, slowly developing crises. It directs you to find the companies that are acutely focused on developing long-term solutions to those problems. Obtaining clean fresh water clearly is going to be a growing problem as far into the future as we can peer. It will require technological solutions such as desalinization to produce scarce fresh water from abundant salt water, infrastructure investments in pipes and pumps to move fresh water from one place to another, and new methods of agriculture and sanitation to use fresh water more efficiently. The best companies in any of those industries—the most profitable, the most innovative, and those with the largest existing market share—will probably perform well over the long term.

Applying the Three Principles of Apocalyptic Investing

It all sounds amazingly simple, doesn't it? But it's still investing, and investing isn't as simple as the old advice "Buy low, sell high." Investing of any sort requires some effort and that's true of investing in the apocalypse too. To use the three principles requires you first to make some judgments about the nature of the cataclysmic event, the likelihood it will occur, the consequences if it does, and how quickly it will play out. Get any of those judgments wrong and you won't realize the full gains that would be possible and may even wind up losing money. One lesson that should be clear when you're thinking about back-door and front-door approaches to making an apocalyptic investment is timing. Some events—a terrorist attack, a pandemic, or a sudden financial meltdown—will require rapid decisions, both about what and when to buy and when to sell. Getting in before the panic is widespread will mean you're buying too high and waiting too long after the event ends, and that may cost you some profits, too.

Other events, such as global warming, the end of easy oil, and, perhaps surprisingly, a collision with an asteroid, will play out over decades if not centuries. You certainly won't need to make snap judgments, but that doesn't mean it will be easy to make the right calls. Given the magnitude of these slowly evolving crises you must understand that governments will play big roles in solving or trying to solve these problems. Understanding the politics of these issues will help you make informed decisions about which companies are worth investing in and which aren't.

You will also need more than a passing grasp of various technologies, from efficient transmission of electricity to techniques for cleaning up coal emissions. Some technologies will sound impressive when reported by the media, but may be too difficult or too expensive to ever be useful. Other seemingly mundane solutions may pack the biggest bang for the buck and thus get the profitable blessing of government funding.

Now you are about to embark on a journey that will take you to some scary places. But once you see how to place these potential catastrophes in their proper perspective, we think they will be a lot less scary. More to the point, we also hope you discover that investing is both an art and a science, and whether you engage in it at Doug's leisurely pace or with James' intensity, it should be both profitable and, dare we say it, a bit of fun?

TWO

PANDEMIC!

I T WILL ALMOST CERTAINLY begin in Southeast Asia, perhaps Vietnam. We'll call her Bian. She's twelve years old, a charming little girl, energetic, bubbling with enthusiasm, and full of love for the little flock of chickens her parents have assigned her to tend. As usual, after collecting some eggs Bian picks up one of her feathered charges and hugs it. At that instant the virus—influenza A type H5N1—makes the leap from the chicken to the little girl. The pandemic has begun.

Bian will have no idea that she has been infected for two or three days. Then after a fitful night of sleep she will tell her mother that she feels bad and will refuse to get out of bed. A little while later she complains that her head hurts and she begins to sweat profusely, the result of a rapidly rising temperature. As the day progresses Bian lies listlessly on her palette. In the afternoon she begins coughing, a deep, hacking cough that causes her to wince with pain. Bian's parents are beginning to get very worried about their little girl, but night is falling and rather than set out for the clinic twenty miles away they decide to nurse her through the night. If she's no better by daybreak they will take her to the nurse at the clinic.

By midnight they regret that decision. Bian has begun vomiting and has a bad case of diarrhea. Her slender little body feels fiery hot to the touch and she's muttering incomprehensibly. The mucus she coughs up is flecked with blood. Her now frantic parents enlist the aid of a neighbor with a car to drive them to the clinic. There they have to ask residents where the nurse lives so that they can awaken her. It takes the nurse only a few minutes to decide that she can do little to help the girl and she instructs the neighbor to drive Bian and her parents to the nearest hospital, some fifty miles away.

As the sun rises the little girl, now lying in a bed surrounded by a small team of doctors and nurses called in when her parents carried her into the hospital lobby, is only semiconscious. The X-rays that are taken as soon as she arrives show an ominous white shadow deep in her right lung, and her breathing crackles when the doctor puts a stethoscope to her chest. She has already been given an injection of an antiviral agent and now the medical team is left to manage her symptoms as best they can.

Their best isn't good enough. After two more days, despite more antiviral drugs and putting the little girl on a respirator,

her lungs are so full of fluid that her skin turns purple from oxygen deprivation. Mercifully she has been unconscious most of the time, but that does little to ease her parents' distress as they watch her gasping futilely for air. Four days after she first complained of a headache, Bian is dead.

The H5N1 virus that killed Bian in a week clearly is extremely lethal. That's because humans have not encountered it before and thus have developed no immunity. But the saving grace had been that the virus had shown little ability to move from one human being to another. The outbreaks that had occurred previously had arisen when members of a family or a village were all exposed to the virus from the flocks of chickens that many rural Southeast Asians depend upon for food and a living. And there, every time in the past, it ended.

But H5N1 is never still. It constantly mutates, and the virus that crossed from the chicken to little Bian was slightly different from the version that caused earlier outbreaks. Its RNA structure was sufficiently different so that it could pass from one human being to another. While Bian coughed and wheezed and vomited she was spraying billions of viral particles into the air around her. Anyone who came near her or cleaned up after her picked up the virus and carried it away from the hospital. They took it home, where they exposed their families, who then carried it to school, to offices, and anywhere else they went. Given the incubation period, of course, no one would realize that the virus was spreading rapidly.

Five days after Bian's death, the husband of one of the nurses who had treated the little girl boarded a plane in Saigon bound

to Los Angeles for training in operating the complex metal-forming equipment his firm had bought. When he boarded the jumbo jet, the virus boarded with him. It would not take investigators from the World Health Organization more than a month to determine that Los Angeles' Bradley International Airport became the initial hub of the pandemic. Flights from Bradley connect to virtually every large city in the world, facilitating the rapid spread of the flu virus.

Within just a few weeks the virulent strain of flu was exploding across the globe, first in the large cities connected by intercontinental airlines, but shortly after in small cities and then into rural areas along major highway routes. The vast network of airplanes, trains, and automobiles that connect the global economy and make travel so fast and efficient have essentially replaced the flocks of rats that spread bubonic plague—the Black Death—throughout Europe in the Middle Ages.

As the flu broke out in first one city, then another, news reports prompted growing alarm. Doctors were quoted saying that they had never encountered such a nasty strain. Rather than infecting the upper portions of victims' respiratory tracts, X-rays were showing that this new flu was penetrating deep into the lungs where it seemed to explode in a matter of hours. Antiviral drugs seemed much less effective against this new strain, and it was proving much more lethal than the usual flu that leaves millions of people feeling tired and achy each year. Now time became essential. People who waited only a day or two to see a physician after feeling symptoms wound up hospi-

talized, many of them on respirators. About half those who were put on respirators died within ten days.

As the extent and lethality of the infection became clear, outright panic set in. People mobbed doctors' offices and hospital emergency rooms, demanding drugs to head off the disease. Even though many advanced countries had stockpiled Tamiflu—the prophylaxis of choice—as well as antiviral drugs, in anticipation of an epidemic, demand quickly outstripped available supply. Governments ordered that the drugs that were on hand were to be used to try to prevent or ameliorate the flu in first responders. Certainly doctors and nurses would have first call on drugs, but so would police as it became evident that desperate crowds seeking protection could quickly get out of control. Hospitals were soon overflowing with desperately ill people. Their supplies of respirators were overwhelmed, and patients who may have been saved instead suffocated as accumulating fluids turned their normally fluffy and resilient lungs into taut bags of liquid through which no oxygen could pass. Not surprisingly, mortuary facilities were soon swamped with corpses. There simply wasn't enough time or space to embalm all the bodies and dig graves, so crematories ran around the clock, seven days a week. In some countries it became necessary to bury the dead in mass graves.

In the initial stages of the pandemic almost everyone was focused on the health effects of the raging disease. The extent of the illness, its ravaging symptoms, and the deaths it caused seemed both physically and psychologically overwhelming. No one seemed safe and that alone was terrifying. But soon the

looming economic and social impact began to become increasingly visible. Parents kept their children out of school, not that it made much difference since so many teachers were sick or dying. Most long-distance travel dried up within a few weeks as people canceled business and pleasure trips to avoid having to breathe the potentially contaminated air circulating in airliners.

Then there were those, mostly residents of big cities who lived in high-rise buildings, who piled their families in cars and struck out for such remote areas as the American southwest in an often futile effort to isolate themselves from the sick or contagious. They were the exception. Tourist destinations were hard hit. Las Vegas's gaudy casinos were silent and their flashing neon lights dark. The high-rise condos that line Miami's oceanfront were empty, and Florida's once-burgeoning tourist attractions shut their doors, not only because there were few tourists, but because so many of their staff were sick. Cruise lines berthed their ships and left aboard only skeleton crews to do minimal maintenance. New York's Broadway was dark. Restaurants, both high-end and fast food, also closed in the face of a dearth of diners. Movie theaters and shopping malls were empty. Sporting events at every level, from high school to professional leagues, were canceled. Grocery stores and drug stores were among the few businesses that continued to attract shoppers, but those who ventured into the stores moved through the aisles quickly wearing rubber gloves and face masks and buying only necessities.

Then absenteeism in offices and factories began to rise sharply. Some people simply wanted to isolate themselves from

any threat from coworkers or customers, but others were either stricken by the virus or attending to ill family members. It wasn't long before assembly lines shut down and businesses restricted entry to mission-critical employees.

Financial markets began to reflect the poisonous effects of the pandemic. Stock prices tumbled amid concerns for future profits even as the price of gold and Treasury bills and bonds soared as perceived safe havens. As factories closed or slowed the prices of most commodities other than gold slumped, reflecting sharply lower demand for steel, copper, and coal. In some smaller nations markets simply ceased trading, although the many electronic exchanges were kept up and running because traders could deal from home through computer networks.

Finally, after several months the pandemic began to ebb. Fewer people were getting sick, and those who had survived a bout with the disease were beginning to regain their strength and were immune to further infection. But the effects of the H5N1 virus continued to ripple through the economy. Many people who had not contracted the disease had focused on caring for their families and had given up or lost jobs as a result. In other families the breadwinner was dead and money was in short supply. Now they had to make important decisions about how to allocate their scarce resources. First it was payments on automobiles and credit cards that became delinquent, then mortgage payments began to slip. Banks began to set aside increasing reserves to cover the mounting losses and became much stricter about lending even though interest rates were near all-time lows that reflected the disinflationary global economy. For many months after the pandemic ended economists worried that the global economy was teetering on the edge of a full-blown long-lasting depression.

The pandemic killed an estimated 120 million people around the globe and cost untold billions. Even years after it struck the effects were still being felt. The loss of so many young people approaching the prime of their lives and careers meant fewer families were formed, birth rates fell, and the demand for housing ebbed. The life insurance companies that survived the wave of claims generated by the pandemic had to recalculate the actuarial equations that underpinned their business. Businesses and governments everywhere had to adjust expectations and planning to reflect the new world that emerged from the pandemic, a world that had changed in ways both large and small.

Investment Implications of a Pandemic

Obviously this futuristic "history" of a global flu pandemic approaches a worst-case scenario. It is entirely possible that the H5N1 virus will never mutate in a way that allows it to spread from one person to another. Even if it does, that mutation may make it much less lethal than it is now. But if there's one thing that we can be fairly certain about, it is that there will be a pandemic of some sort. Global travel and the concentration of so many people in big cities around the world make it almost inevitable that some bug will get loose and wreak havoc around the world. With that unfortunate scenario looming before us, what's an investor to do?

Let's take this back to basic investment principles. While a pandemic is serious business, one thing we do know is that there will be more pandemics predicted than there will be actual pandemics. And in an actual pandemic, there will be fewer lives lost than were initially predicted. So let's take our general principles described in chapter 1 and outline how they should be applied to the topic of pandemics.

Principle One: Fade the Fear

Every few years we see the whiff of a pandemic. In 2002 everyone was worried about the bioterrorist threat of an anthrax pandemic that never arrived. In early 2003, it was SARS. People began wearing gas masks to work, productivity slowed, airlines literally halted going in and out of Hong Kong. The economic malaise was so great that, in addition to the onset of the Iraq War, the bull market that began in 2003 seemed to be in jeopardy.

But of course the world did not end. March and April of 2003, when the SARS fears were at their peak, turned out to be the best time to buy the market for the next five years. According to CDC.gov, a total of 8,908 people contracted the SARS virus worldwide between November 2002 and June 2003. Of those, 774 died and no new cases were reported after July 2003. While we offer our condolences to the families of those who died, the simple fact is that the impact of the "pandemic" simply wasn't severe enough to cause a global economic slowdown.

H1N1, however, was a much more serious problem as demonstrated by these statistics from the U.S. Centers for Disease Control:

- Between 42 million and 86 million cases of 2009 H1N1 occurred between April 2009 and February 13, 2010.

- Between 188,000 and 389,000 H1N1-related hospitalizations occurred between April 2009 and February 13, 2010.

- Between about 8,520 and 17,620 H1N1-related deaths occurred between April 2009 and February 13, 2010.

Despite those frightening numbers, however, the panic again was overrated. The symptoms of swine flu include a runny nose, fever, coughing, headache, chills, and fatigue, pretty much the same array of symptoms that most strains of flu produce. The primary difference between swine flu and the flu we normally contract was that swine flu was immune to the vaccine that had been produced to avoid the regular flu. In other words, there was little protection against this mutated flu, and that scared people and also scared the markets. Headlines began to spread almost as quickly as the flu itself: "WHO raises swine flu alert level" was a *USA Today* headline in April 2009. "WHO declares pandemic" was a June 2009 headline in the *Independent* in the U.K. "India should brace for swine flu pandemic" was an August 2009 headline in the *Daily Times*. Pandemic headlines became a media pandemic.

The fear became more pervasive than the illness itself. So rule number one in our general principles for dealing with a world-ending catastrophe is to "fade the fear." Fear begets opportunity, and as we see throughout this book, the best buying opportunities occur when the rest of the world is running scared. Any irrational seller of stock will be met by a rational buyer.

How does one fade the fear in the case of pandemics? Should we just buy the general market if it dips? That's one possibility. The general market is best represented by the Spyders Exchange Traded Fund which carries the ticker symbol, SPY. This ETF is an aggregation of all five hundred companies in the S&P 500. When it or the S&P 500 falls as a result of apparently irrational fear, it's time to jump in with both feet.

But a pandemic also allows us to become more focused on our investments. In the case of SARS, the market that was most affected was Hong Kong, where the SARS virus was first quarantined. On March 31, 2003, the Hong Kong Department of Health began quarantining specific streets in order to prevent the spread of the virus. This was a first and quickly led to fears that travel in and out of Hong Kong would cause worldwide spread of the virus. This, of course, led to panic in the Hong Kong stock markets.

While the U.S. markets had already begun recovering from the dot-com bust of 2000–2—reaching a low point in March 2003 that was not seen again until 2009—the Hong Kong market did not reach its low point until mid-April, as can be seen in the following chart:

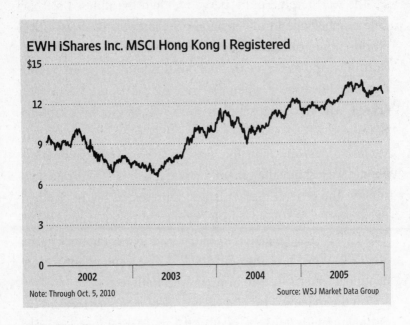

EWH iShares Inc. MSCI Hong Kong I Registered

Note: Through Oct. 5, 2010   Source: WSJ Market Data Group

The chart is of EWH, which is the exchange traded fund representing the Hong Kong market. EWH reached a low on April 23, 2003, at 6.55 and then began a sharp year-long recovery, snapping back even faster than the U.S. market. While it's hard to predict a bottom, and we're not recommending that you should buy all the way down, it's always worthwhile to identify the markets that are being affected the most by the fear of world destruction, take a position in that market, and wait it out. The results, as we showed in chapter 1, are almost always gratifying in the long run and sometimes in the short run.

Principle Two: Invest through the Back Door

When a pandemic fear occurs, regardless of whether it is a real threat to the world, billions of dollars will be spent trying to cure the virus or other cause. As we explained in chapter 1, this situation affords investors two routes to take advantage of the situation: a "front-door" approach and a "back-door" approach. The front-door approach involves stocks of companies whose entire purpose is to cure a specific illness. The back-door approach involves stocks in companies that have multiple product lines, only one of which is aimed at curing or preventing the cause of the pandemic. We tend to advocate the back-door approach. It's safer, but still takes advantage of the inherent fear that will sweep the globe as a pandemic emerges and expands.

A particularly attractive facet of the back-door approach is that it doesn't require you to wait to seize the moment when panic strikes. Instead, you can make your investment now or at any point in the future, confident that over time a pandemic or at least the fear of a pandemic will emerge and your investment will rise. We're talking, of course, about the behemoth billion-dollar pharmaceutical companies that are the prime beneficiaries of any worries about pandemics. It may not be their only business, but it becomes an important part of their business to deliver vaccines that work, are safe, and can be produced quickly, whenever a pandemic occurs. These stocks will not go down with the rest of the market, and the more real the fears are, the more likely these stocks will go up significantly.

It's a great example of how actually owning stocks is a better method of hedging than shorting stocks. It just depends on what stocks you own. Generally, owning a basket of pharmaceutical companies that work on cures for the many ills afflicting humanity—and generating billions of profits in the process—will almost certainly pose no risk of being wiped out, pandemic or not. If a pandemic occurs, you stand to reap significant profits.

With flu pandemics—the most likely to occur—it is worth remembering that there are two antiviral medicines out there that are used to treat the flu: Tamiflu, distributed by Roche, a Swiss-based pharmaceutical giant, and the antiviral drug Relenza, which is distributed by GlaxoSmithKline. Roche's stock doesn't trade in the United States, but Gilead Sciences, which actually developed Tamiflu and gets a 20% royalty payment on all units of the medicine sold, is based in the United States and trades under the symbol GILD. GlaxoSmithKline is listed as GSK.

We are not necessarily recommending these stocks, but they do represent our second principle at work: they are profitable, successful companies that also have a handle on curing the world threat. In 2009, GILD, for instance, had $7 billion in revenues, $2.6 billion in profits, and experienced 43% revenue growth. In addition to its royalty payments on Tamiflu (which represent about 12% of its profits), it also has an approximate 75% market share in drugs for the HIV/AIDS virus, and it has been making steady inroads in the Hepatitis B, cystic fibrosis, and other markets.

GlaxoSmithKline, in addition to making Relenza, which is

used to treat the flu, also makes a flu vaccine and is one of the few companies approved for a swine flu vaccine in the United States. The other influenza vaccine makers are AstraZeneca, Novartis, and SanofiAventis. A basket of all of the stocks might be a good, somewhat diversified way of hedging against the threat of a flu pandemic while also making a long-term investment on the rise in healthcare with an aging baby boomer population. We say "somewhat diversified" because while we are not diversifying away country risk, we are diversifying away management risk if any of the individual companies falter.

Glaxo is a megabehemoth with over $43 billion in revenues and $8.4 billion in profits in 2009, a 60% year-over-year earnings growth. The range of its products is immense, and an investment in Glaxo would serve two purposes. First, it is a front-door approach to buying a stock simply because the company is growing; it is safe (GSK has an enormous cash position and little debt); and it has the demographic winds at its back as the world lives longer and needs more cures for more ills. At the same time it is a back-door approach to reaping the benefits of increased expenditures on both antivirals and flu vaccines. If an actual pandemic occurs, and we certainly hope it doesn't, GlaxoSmithKline will make enormous revenues and profits, making the company the ideal hedge against such a cataclysmic event.

Principle Three: Invest through the Front Door

For principle three you want to identify the stocks whose entire reason for being is to solve the issue of the threat being posed. These are often very speculative plays that can be thought of as one-trick ponies. Since they are speculative they have the opportunity for enormous gains but also could be zeroes. A great example (discussed in another chapter) was Invision after 9/11. Trading around $1 at the time, near the levels of the cash it had in the bank (meaning the market was valuing its business at almost zero), Invision was a one-trick pony that relied on airports and the government using it to build explosive detection equipment at every airport. This was enough to carry the stock from single digits before 9/11 to being acquired by GE a few years later for $50. You could've bought the stock the day after 9/11, even after it had already soared 100%, and still had returns of 400% before it was eventually acquired a few years later.

There are many small, speculative biotech stocks that are working on vaccines for future generations of the flu. You shouldn't necessarily buy these to hedge against future fears of a pandemic (it would be better to use principle #2 to hedge), but when hint of a pandemic occurs it would be interesting to buy a basket of these (or a basket of any new stocks out there that are working on the latest cures because some of the stocks mentioned here will probably be either out of business or acquired).

BioCryst Pharmaceuticals (BCRX) is in various FDA trials

for drugs that treat viral infections. This company is in its early stages and should be around for the next several iterations of pandemic fears.

As can be seen on the chart below, you would not have wanted to own this stock in anticipation of a pandemic but once the fears started to surface of people being infected by a new virus that was immune to prior vaccine treatments, BCRX would've been a good stock to own:

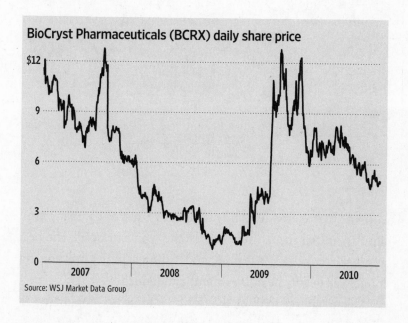

BioCryst Pharmaceuticals (BCRX) daily share price

Source: WSJ Market Data Group

Vical Inc. (VICL) has another drug that is in the middle of various preclinical trials for various pandemic vaccines. Again, the stock was a nothing until the H1N1 fears surfaced and then the stock moved steadily up until it started to settle down to earth (precisely when people were no longer as concerned with H1N1):

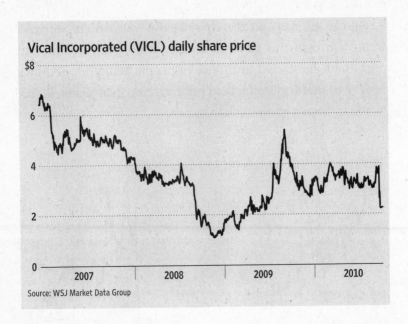

Vical Incorporated (VICL) daily share price

Source: WSJ Market Data Group

Note that there was plenty of time to buy this company even after its initial move up and after the fears surfaced. The best approach is buying a basket and riding it out until you no longer see deadly headlines about pandemics.

A good source to track the fear on a topic is Google Trends, found at trends.google.com. This service provided by Google tracks the usage of a certain search phrase on Google over time. See the Google Trends chart for H1N1.

When the virus surfaced in early 2009, it was a good time to begin accumulating the speculative basket. And when the trend turned down sharply in October 2009, it was a good

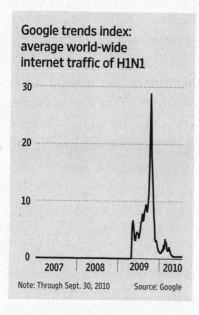

Google trends index: average world-wide internet traffic of H1N1

Note: Through Sept. 30, 2010

Source: Google

time to exit the speculative portion of the trade—the front-door stocks devoted solely to a cure, as opposed to the larger, more diversified stocks.

One other front-door company that is a play on pandemics, but not as speculative as a biotech company that requires enormous amounts of cash to make its way through trials, is Alpha Pro Technologies.

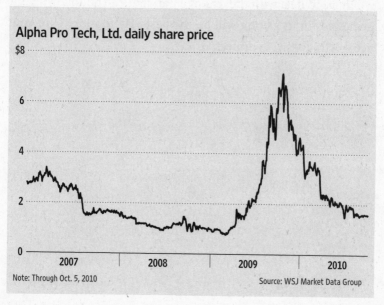

Alpha Pro Tech, Ltd. daily share price

Note: Through Oct. 5, 2010

Source: WSJ Market Data Group

We've seen the same pattern we see in APT in the above two stocks as well. The steady rise when the first fears of pandemic arose, and then the slow sell-off once the fears peaked.

What does the company do? It makes the surgical masks that people wear when they want to avoid the kinds of infection that can be picked up from breathing the air on a crowded city street, in a building, or under the ground in a subway. The company was a huge winner in the pandemic fears of 2009, with revenues up over 100% and earnings up over 1000%. The stock will settle down, but the next time the world is sweating at every sign of infection, there is little doubt that this stock will make its move again.

We hope we never have to deal with a serious pandemic of the sort that hit the world in 1918. But we know for a fact we will have to deal with the fear of a pandemic. And following the principles in this book will be the best way to make sure your net worth doesn't get infected.

THREE

NOR ANY DROP TO DRINK

The Emerging Fresh Water Crisis

T HE TALE IS ALL too common throughout the Third World. Water systems are inadequate to serve the population of the largest cities and even the wealthiest neighborhoods. Raw sewage flows into rivers and streams. Industrial plants dump toxic chemicals into those same rivers or onto the ground where they seep into local water supplies, causing disease that kills people, plants, and animals. Farmers desperate to irrigate their crops draw water from rivers, often extracting so much that only a mere trickle, and sometimes not even that, makes it to the mouth where the once mighty rivers flowed into the ocean. Wells to supply water both for drinking and irrigation dry up as underground reservoirs are drained. People dig the wells deeper to reach the remaining water, but that, too, eventually disappears. Eventually productive agricultural land returns to wilderness as the farmers move away to seek other employment.

A grim scenario, no doubt about it. But this isn't some Third World nation we're talking about, it's the United States of America. And it is a tale that is being repeated all over the globe, from the sophisticated cities of Europe to the frantically industrializing regions of China, India, Brazil, and almost every other country in the world. Individually and together, the nations of the world are rushing headlong toward a fresh water crisis, a shortage of what is, after the air we breathe, the single most important chemical for life on Earth in all its forms. The frightening fact is the world is running out of clean water and that will have enormous consequences. Even as we write this over 50% of the hospital beds worldwide are filled by someone suffering from an illness related to dirty water. As emerging nations develop, the trend of rural workers moving to urban areas is only increasing the demand for water while little is done to increase the supply. By 2020, the UN estimates that close to 40% of the world's population will be without adequate clean water. This is a problem that is only going to get worse and significant money will be spent solving this issue.

The problem has multiple sources. It begins with the fact that while 70% of the Earth's surface consists of water, 97% of that water is salt water, leaving just 3% in the form of fresh water. Of that paltry amount, more than two thirds is locked up in icecaps and glaciers. Another 30% is in underground aquifers. Just 1% is in the form of surface water: lakes, rivers, and swamps.

That 1% of the world's water that is both fresh and usable has been carrying an ever-increasing burden as the world's population has grown. Agriculture was and still is the biggest use of fresh water, with an estimated 69% of available fresh water being used for crops. Those crops, in turn, become food for human beings or for the animals they raise for food. The good news is that agriculture has met the challenge of feeding a population that has more than doubled from 3 billion in 1960 to nearly 7 billion. The number of people suffering from hunger in that time span has been halved. The bad news is that the world's population is projected to grow to nearly 10 billion by 2050, and the gap between available water supply and water demand clearly will limit future expansion of irrigation to grow crops.

Industry accounts for an estimated 15% of worldwide water use, at least some (a tiny portion) of which is salt water used to cool power plants situated in coastal areas. Hydropower created by damming rivers and forcing water through turbines is another significant use of water. While it seems superficially good that people can tap a clean source of energy through hydropower, the problem is that the vast reservoirs behind those dams allow much more water to be lost through evaporation than was lost when the rivers were running free. The result? The flow downstream from the dams is less than it was before they were built. But the real industrial culprit in the developing fresh water crisis is pollution in the form of waste products dumped directly into fresh water sources or onto the ground where toxins percolate into underground aquifers and wells.

Households use most of the remaining 15% of worldwide water for drinking, bathing, cooking, and sanitation. While amounts vary from one nation to another the average global per capita use of water amounts to more than thirteen gallons a day. Unfortunately not everyone has access to clean fresh water, and many people end up drinking, cooking, and bathing with water contaminated with toxic chemicals, bacteria, or viruses. And without dedicated sources of clean fresh water to drink, it's pretty certain that the human wastes those same people produce each day flush directly into a river, lake, or underground aquifer to further contaminate what fresh water there is—a vicious cycle of disease and death.

To use water, whether for agriculture, industry, or household needs, there must be a way to get the water from where it is to where it is required. Buckets serve that purpose in many villages in developing countries, but most of the developed world has hundreds of thousands of miles of pipes to move water from its source to users. Many of those water systems were built years ago, however, sometimes centuries ago. Pipes develop leaks that either result in water lost in transit or contaminated by chemicals or biological agents. Cities all over the world face this problem of aging, failing water systems. But because people have become accustomed to nearly cost-free water supplied reliably (less so today than forty years ago) to their homes and businesses, governments are having a hard time convincing their constituents that their water rates need to rise significantly to fund the billions of dollars that will be necessary to overhaul these systems.

And once water has been used for some purposes—bathing, sanitation, cooking, or in industrial processes—it must be carried off. In the slums of New Delhi it is carried off in open gutters that pervade the shanties with stench and bacterial contamination. In modern cities in the United States and Europe, it is carried away in the same kinds of pipes that delivered it. Much of it is taken to treatment facilities where it is at least partially sanitized before it is returned to a river or stream. But as population growth puts increased pressure on these aging sewage systems, they can be overtaxed, especially during hard rains. Pipes rupture, or the treatment system simply can't handle the excessive flow, and raw sewage gets dumped into a waterway.

Round and Round She Goes: The Water Cycle

For the most part water is neither created nor destroyed, but it does change forms and is highly mobile. It is in short supply in some places while other places have ample amounts, and it is pricey for us to move. Water infrastructure—reservoirs to collect it, pipes and pumps to move it into cities and fields and out to sanitation facilities—is enormously expensive, and, problematically, the price people have been willing to pay for water has been very small. As the Earth's climate changes, meteorologists warn us that we will see more droughts, more floods, melting glaciers, and rising sea levels. Put another way, we will have water—just not where we want it or need it.

Because the water cycle—known more technically as the "hydrologic cycle"—has neither a beginning nor an end, we can join it at any point. Let's start with surface water in Lake Mead, the gigantic reservoir created in the 1930s by the construction of the massive Hoover Dam across the Colorado River. Lake Mead extends 112 miles behind the dam and its shores touch both Arizona and Nevada. It supplies millions of people in those states with both drinking water and hydroelectric power. Without the dam and lake (and Lake Powell behind the Glen Canyon Dam farther downstream on the Colorado River), those areas would be unable to support anything remotely approaching the current population. But situated as it is in a desert, the waters of Lake Mead are highly susceptible to evaporation, much more so than the Colorado River itself was before the Hoover Dam was built. Combined with similar evaporation from Lake Powell evaporation accounts for about 10% of the Colorado River's annual flow.

Evaporated water suspended in the Earth's atmosphere goes where the wind takes it and eventually forms clouds that further condense and provide rain or snow. But the evaporated water doesn't always return as rain or snow to a place where it can flow back downhill and replenish Lake Mead. When that happens the combined effects of evaporation, the flow of water through the Hoover Dam's hydroelectric plant, and the extraction of water to water lawns and brew coffee for millions of people living in the desert around Lake Mead, draws down the volume of the lake. As demand grows from more extensive agriculture and a swelling population in places like Las Vegas, some hydrologists are beginning to predict that some time in the next forty years the lake's volume will drop to the point where it will no longer drive the Hoover Dam's turbines.

Outside of big cities wells are often the source of water for both human consumption and irrigation. Wells tap the underground water in an aquifer—a strata of porous rock, often limestone. But the replenishment of an aquifer from rain can occur much more slowly than water is withdrawn from wells. When that happens the water table—the height of water in the aquifer—begins to fall. Wells must be dug deeper to tap the remaining water. And withdrawing all that water from an aquifer can damage it. In Florida, surrounded on three sides by salt water, the fresh water used to keep all those golf courses and lawns green comes from an aquifer in which salt water is gradually intruding to replace the extracted fresh water. In other aquifers the extraction of water allows the weight of the overburden to crush and compress the porous rock, leaving it incapable of ever holding as much water as it once did.

To add another layer of complexity to the water cycle we need to take a closer look at agricultural use of water. David Pimentel, professor of ecology at Cornell University's College of Agriculture and Life Sciences, estimates that to grow one pound of potatoes requires around 60 gallons of water. The same amount of wheat requires 108 gallons and a pound of rice sucks up as much as 230 gallons of water. But what is really shocking is that the quarter-pounder hamburger you had for lunch took 3,000 gallons of water to produce. These facts, while basic, are important for investors to understand because they help us recognize which companies are intimately tied to the drinkable water crisis and why.

Investment Implications of Dwindling Supplies of Fresh Water

The world's growing lack of clean water is being propelled by three global demographic changes:

- The population is growing and every human being needs water.

- Industry and manufacturing is growing and most industries need water.

- More people are moving from rural areas to urban areas and that will require moving water to satisfy their thirst.

The United Nations is predicting that the lack of clean water will become catastrophic during the next thirty years. That dire forecast virtually guarantees that large sums of money will be spent on fresh water. A Credit Suisse report on the water industry identifies four categories of spending in the quest for "blue gold":

- **Activities and technologies that increase supply.** This category refers to recycling water so it can be used again, or desalination that converts salt water to potable fresh water. Recycled water is mostly used for industrial purposes since it's unlikely to be drinkable.

- **The building of the necessary water infrastructure.** This category includes the building of facilities for clean water management, dams to capture and store water, and pipelines to take water to the people who need it. It also includes the development of better technology to prevent leaks in the pipelines and the production of packaged water.

- **Processes that help reduce demand.** This category mostly refers to industrial and agricultural processes, although improved home plumbing can contribute.

- **Water management.** This term refers to the overall concept of applying the first three.

Rather than dividing companies by our three principles of apocalyptic investing, the approach we recommend for dealing with the demise of clean water worldwide is to build a basket of solid, growing companies that are diversified according to each of the four categories described above from the Credit Suisse report.

Desalination companies are one obvious play to solve the supply side of the problem. With 97% of the world's water supply in oceans, the process of getting rid of the salt will be in increasing demand. But aging pipes that leak billions of gallons of water each year are another obvious target for increasing supplies of fresh water.

As usual, General Electric is the biggest desalination company in the space but since water revenues are only about 10% of GE's revenues it's worth looking elsewhere for more bang for your fresh water buck. Energy Recovery (ERII) is a pure front-door play in the desalination space. It provides a key energy component in desalination plants and has a solid backlog of orders. Additionally, it has a stellar balance sheet ($80 million cash, no debt) and is profitable. Warren Buffett always says the best investments are the ones that you know will be there ten years from now. This company will certainly exist ten years from now on the basis of the strong water trend, the great balance sheet, the enormous backlog, and its current profitability. Companies like this usually get acquired before they have a chance to fully flourish, but for now this company is operating independently. Consolidated Water Company (CWCO) is also a pure front-door play on desalination with a focus on the Caribbean.

Danaher (DHR) is a miniconglomerate in the water testing business. The company manufactures and markets a range of analytical instruments, related consumables, and associated services that detect and measure chemical, physical, and microbiological parameters in water. Nalco (NLC) provides the chemicals that are used in water purification. Among other things, Nalco chemicals are useful in cleaning up water affected by oil spills.

Jacobs Engineering (JEC) is an engineering firm that makes everything from oil rigs to wastewater treatment plants. While most of its revenues at the moment come from the oil services side of its business, it's a good back-door way to play the water business.

Donaldson Company has seen its profits grow for nearly two decades, through three recessions including the last one. The company makes liquid filtration systems (used for recycling water), air filtration systems, and emission control systems. Liquid filtration systems make up about 15% of Donaldson's revenues. Other than a small blip during the last recession, the stock returns have been steady and impressive.

Donaldson Company, Inc. daily share price

Note: Through Oct. 5, 2010   Source: WSJ Market Data Group

Ashland Inc. (ASH) is a specialty chemicals company whose chemicals treat wastewater from industrial processes so that it can be recycled through the process. But unlike Donaldson, Ashland was vulnerable to the most recent financial panic. You can see in the accompanying chart that Ashland got whacked in late 2008 and early 2009. In hindsight we are certain that the plunge marked a tremendous buying opportunity to pick up shares of a company that is likely to post some healthy long-term profits dealing with the water situation.

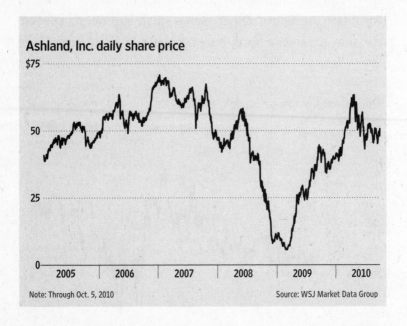

Ashland, Inc. daily share price

Note: Through Oct. 5, 2010

Source: WSJ Market Data Group

To treat water you not only need chemicals, you also need the pumps, valves, and pipes to get water through the treatment system. Flowserve (FLS) has the admirable task of making heavy-duty pumps. The good thing about selling the pumps and valves is that Flowserve also is the most qualified company to maintain them. About 40% of Flowserve's revenues (and a larger than 40% chunk of their profits, due to the margins on support services) come from ongoing maintenance fees.

There are several other attractive companies in this "picks and shovels" sector of the water category, including Crane Co. (CR), which makes valves and pumps that are used in water treatment facilities. This is a company that is unlikely to disappear. Started in 1855, it has survived multiple depressions and recessions and has a diversified product offering, making everything from vending machines to aircraft landing systems. That said, it's the water side of the business that will be its biggest growth engine as the world continues its steady decline of clean water. Others include Idex Corp. (IEX), which makes pump products, and Mueller Water Products (MWA), which makes valves and pipes. Finally, Insituform (INSU) provides processes that fix leaking supply pipes without having to dig them up.

All the above companies address the supply side of the water equation. Monsanto is a back-door play on addressing the demand side of the water equation. Monsanto is working on seeds that will grow drought-resistant corn and cotton. In trials, corn using the Monsanto process had a 6%–10% greater yield given the same amount of water.

Finally, amid all this talk of supply and demand we need to look at the price of water. While many people think water is virtually free, the facts tell a different story. The price of water is exceeding the pace of inflation and if that trend continues, as we expect it will, it bodes well for the companies that actually deliver water to our homes. A representative sampling of private water utilities includes American States Water Company (AWR) based in California; Connecticut Water Services (CTWS), providing water in Connecticut and Massachusetts; Philadelphia Suburban (PSC), serving the East Coast; and Southwest Water Company (SWWC), which provides water in twenty-nine states. Like their cousins in the electric utility space, these water utilities provide a nice flow of dividends, usually averaging about 3%, well above the return on T-bills.

Finally, the ultimate back-door play is Coca-Cola. Thanks to its purchase of VitaminWater, Coca-Cola is a major player in the bottled water space. Of course, Coca-Cola's bread and butter is its carbonated beverage business, but as people become more health conscious the demand for bottled water is on the rise.

FOUR

TOUGH OIL

B Y ANY STANDARDS TRANSOCEAN LTD.'S Deepwater Horizon was a tremendous feat of engineering. Designed to drill down 30,000 feet for oil in ocean depths up to 8,000 feet, the immense rig was 396 feet long and 256 feet wide. Eight engines rated at 7,375 horsepower each turned big propellers that could rotate 360 degrees to keep the semisubmersible rig precisely stationed over the drill hole. It could operate in twenty-nine-foot seas and was designed to survive waves in excess of forty-one feet and hurricane-force winds of more than one hundred miles an hour.

In the spring of 2010 Deepwater Horizon was on lease for several hundred thousand dollars a day to BP Group, one of the world's largest oil companies, and was drilling for oil in the

Gulf of Mexico forty-one miles off the coast of Louisiana. The weather Tuesday night, April 20, was good, operations were going well, and among the 126-member crew aboard the rig who weren't working, some were watching television while others were sacked out in their bunks to grab some sleep. At about 10 p.m. a tremendous explosion rocked the giant rig, and a raging fire followed. The U.S. Coast Guard responded immediately with cutters and helicopters, taking off 115 crewmembers, 17 of whom were taken immediately to shoreside hospitals to be treated for injuries ranging from minor to severe. Eleven crewmen simply disappeared and were never found.

The oil-fueled fire burned for a day and half despite heroic efforts to quell it. Then at midmorning Thursday, April 22, another blast rang out over the Gulf of Mexico and the giant rig toppled and sank. A day later the Coast Guard said there was no evidence that any oil was leaking from the well head, but that assessment changed the next day when remote submersible craft found oil gushing from leaks in a drilling pipe almost a mile below the surface. The gusher continued unabated for nearly three months, dumping an estimated five million barrels of oil into the Gulf of Mexico and contaminating hundreds of miles of fertile marshlands that were a home and breeding ground to millions of fish and fowl. Commercial fishing and oystering, the economic lifeblood of Louisiana's southern bayous, was banned in large swatches of the Gulf of Mexico. The well was eventually plugged, but the full effects of the Gulf spill are currently unknowable.

There will be many recriminations and much second-guessing of what could or should have been done to prevent the massive spill or to minimize its effects. Litigation will continue for years. Government policy on offshore drilling will be in flux for the foreseeable future. But the lesson for us in the Gulf of Mexico oil spill goes far beyond the precise cause of the disaster. Rather, the explosion of Deepwater Horizon demonstrates the good news and the bad news about our global dependence on oil to drive industrial economies.

First, the good news: the world won't run out of oil during our lifetimes.

The bad news: the world *will* run out of easily obtained oil. Soon.

The essential problem is that the world's big oil companies have apparently found and are currently exploiting all the easy-to-get oil. Mankind has been using crude oil for centuries as a medicinal agent, for illumination, and for machinery lubrication. But until the mid-1800s they had never sought it in a systematic way, instead stumbling on "seeps," crevasses, and fissures in the earth's surface that allowed subterranean oil deposits to slowly percolate to the surface. One of the biggest and best-known seeps was in northwestern Pennsylvania, but it was initially considered an irritant. Farmers and landowners drilling water wells kept penetrating oil reservoirs that contaminated the water they needed for drinking and irrigation. Then in 1859 Edwin Drake drilled a well specifically to tap the subsurface oil. As the commercial potential of crude oil became clear, the global quest for oil began.

Pennsylvania may have first claim as the place where oil became a commercially viable product, but Texas holds the title as the birthplace of the modern oil industry. On January 10, 1901, after months of backbreaking drilling on a hill in southeastern Texas called Spindletop that had yielded only minute quantities of oil, the workmen were lowering their drill back into a drilled shaft that was 1,020 feet. It had been seventeen hours since any drilling had taken place in the shaft, but suddenly oily mud began burbling to the surface of the hole. Then with a furious burst, the heavy drill shaft was blown out of the hole. Nothing else happened for several minutes. Then, with a loud blast, mud, gas and oil began spewing into the air from the drill hole. The plume of crude oil shot up more than 150 feet, twice the height of the drill derrick. It was the world's first man-made "gusher," and it flowed at the astounding rate of one hundred thousand barrels per day, more than the combined flow from all the existing wells in the United States.

The success of the purposeful exploration for oil in the United States touched off a global search for more sources of petroleum. Only a few years after the Spindletop gusher erupted it was becoming increasingly apparent that the Middle East had huge oil resources. But it wasn't until after World War II that serious exploration and exploitation of Middle East oil began. By 1960, when Iran, Iraq, Kuwait, Saudi Arabia, and Venezuela formed the Organization of the Petroleum Exporting Countries (OPEC), it was absolutely clear that the Middle East sat astride the world's greatest deposits of crude oil. But those Middle Eastern deposits weren't the only ones, just the largest. Since then big reserves were found in the North Sea and on Alaska's North Slope. The oceans are still in the early stages of exploration and exploitation. But these more recent discoveries illustrate the problem: extracting large amounts of oil from the Alaskan wilderness and the dangerous North Sea has been neither cheap nor easy. And as the Deepwater Horizon disaster illustrates, tapping the oil reservoirs beneath the oceans will be even more difficult and expensive.

The development of new petroleum discoveries tends to follow the same pattern. At first the newly discovered oil is easy to tap. The drillers at Spindletop were confronted with the problem of how to harness the raging gusher, not how to pull the oil out of the ground. As the geology of a new discovery becomes clearer and additional wells are drilled, production from an oil field continues to increase over a period ranging from a few to many years. But at some point the easy oil is gone. The field still holds lots of petroleum, but getting it from the reservoir to the surface becomes more difficult. The daily flow of each well decreases and new wells drilled in other parts of the reservoir don't flow nearly as fast as the earliest wells. Eventually the flow slows to the point that the oil company begins to take new measures to extract the oil. Water or steam injection may be used to pressurize the underground reservoir and drive more oil to the surface. Finally there comes a day when further exploitation is simply too difficult or expensive given the price of a barrel of oil. Many of the Texas oil fields that were so productive in the first half of the last century are either depleted today or will be in the near future.

Unfortunately, the global pattern of oil exploitation follows that same course. New oil is easy to extract at first, and production builds over time, but eventually all the easy oil is gone. Today we know that production rates of the Middle East's vast reservoirs, as well as those of Alaska and the North Sea, are declining. The question is when, not if, we reach a condition that experts call "peak oil." That's when global oil production reaches the highest level it ever will. Some experts believe we have already reached that point, others that peak oil may still be twenty or more years away. But whenever peak oil occurs, production of petroleum will gradually decline. How fast it declines is a matter of much conjecture. Some estimates are as low as 2% per year, some posit 5% per year, and the most alarmist projections are 13% a year. But regardless of how fast production declines, the supply of oil runs head-on into the really alarming problem: population growth and oil use are increasing rapidly with no signs of abating anytime soon. Billions of new drivers and millions of new cars will be hitting the road as China and India—among other places—industrialize and become, like the United States, Europe, and Japan before them, mobile nations. The upshot is that demand for oil will far outstrip supply. And in classical economics that means only one thing: higher prices.

As people become more willing to pay higher prices for gasoline and other petroleum byproducts, the world's oil companies will push harder to extract oil from the deepest oceans and from the shale and tar sands that hold immense amounts of petroleum locked up in their geological structures. But that will only be feasible at much higher prices than the world is now paying for a barrel of oil. Think of rising oil prices as an industrial tax and an increasingly heavy one at that. As we have learned—but not necessarily retained—from previous "oil shocks," higher energy prices slow economic growth. How high oil prices rise and how soon will determine the impact of peak oil on the world economy. If prices rise gradually, perhaps the world economy can adapt with minimal disruption. But if prices rise suddenly for any number of reasons, the economic effects could be devastating, especially in advanced countries. The trouble is, we're not well equipped to make those predictions about how fast prices will rise mostly because we don't have very good information about how much oil is still reasonably easy to access. Both oil producing countries and the oil companies themselves are notoriously unreliable in disclosing their reserves.

Another factor in trying to predict what will happen to oil supplies and prices is the uncertainty about the economic effects of rising oil prices and how quickly the world can adapt. The Great Economic Collapse of 2008 and the global recession it caused put a big dent in oil demand. And $4-a-gallon gas in the United States in 2007 effectively became a great advertising campaign to help Toyota launch its Prius hybrid gasoline-electric car. Today all the major automakers are rushing to produce hybrid or all-electric vehicles in anticipation of rising oil prices.

Oil consumption is also tied to the problems of global climate change and we can't predict how government policies around the world to deal with climate warming will affect taxes and prices of various energy sources, although it is almost certain that wind, solar, and nuclear power cannot fully substitute for oil in the world's industrialized economy. A final uncertainty about oil surrounds the conflict between what is essentially a bloc made of the Western economies and Japan on one side and the Islamic nations on the other, the outcome of which is impossible to predict—assuming that there will be an outcome and not just a prolonged battle that extends beyond the foreseeable future.

The only thing that is certain is that over time oil prices will rise, which is the same thing as saying oil will become a more valuable commodity. Perhaps the silver lining in the very dark cloud sewn by the Deepwater Horizon disaster was President Obama's reversal of his decision to open East Coast waters to oil exploration. Now whatever oil is under those ocean waters will remain there, growing in value over time.

Investment Implications of Peak Oil

Many of us with a few years under our expanding belts recall the Oil Shock of 1973. It was the first really dramatic economic crisis to confront us since the Great Depression. People sat in their cars for hours in lines miles long to get to the gasoline pumps at service stations, all for the privilege of filling the tanks of their gas guzzlers with gasoline that cost four times as much as it had just a few weeks earlier. All that panic was created when OPEC cut production by a mere 5%, sending oil prices to what at the time was an astounding level of $12 a barrel from $3.

There was no geological reason for the 1973 oil shock. Rather it was political. First, it was punishment directed at the United States for lending support to Israel in the Yom Kippur War that started in October 1973 when Egypt and Syria attempted to invade Israel. Second, it was a counterpunch. The United States had been pressuring the oil exporting countries to keep their price increases at no more than 2% a year. Yet the prices of products we sold them had been rising at a much faster rate because of our big inflation problems. Wheat, for example, nearly doubled in price in 1973.

The 5% increase in oil prices triggered a panic in 1973 because our demand for oil was insatiable. Unfortunately, it still is.

Yet while our demand for oil is insatiable, we can see the future in our own supply and demand for the liquid gold. In 1970 the United States produced about ten million barrels per day. Today that production is halved, to about five million barrels per day. In 1970 we could just about supply our own needs of a little more than ten million barrels per day. Now we consume twice as much. As a result we are today undertaking what legendary oil baron T. Boone Pickens describes as "the greatest transfer of wealth mankind has ever seen" as more of our dollars than ever are sent to the Middle East to pay for oil.

We all know that supply and demand determine the price of a commodity. If supply is 85 million barrels a day given the global oil industry's current technology and resources, we need to examine the demand side of the equation. We need the energy derived from oil for transportation and to power our homes, businesses, and factories. Today demand for oil is about 86 million barrels a day. Estimates are that by 2030 our demand for oil will increase 37% to 118 million barrels a day. These estimates factor in the growth of demand in industrialized countries like the United States, the growth in developing countries like China, and general population growth. If these numbers continue as predicted, we're clearly in for some problems very soon.

China and India in particular have seen spikes in their demand for oil. In the past ten years Chinese consumption of oil has grown from 3.5 million barrels a day to over seven million barrels a day, while the United States has gone from 17.7 million barrels a day to 20 million barrels. In 2008 alone, China experienced 15% growth in automobile sales, signaling that future demand for oil will most likely continue to increase. India also has more than doubled oil consumption since 2002 and is expected to be up to 5 million barrels a day by 2030.

Long-term Solutions?

The world has long been aware that oil is getting tougher to extract and the price is rising. The result is increasing interest in ways to mitigate the supply and price problems looming in the near future. None come without their own problems, and all should be kept in mind as you make investment decisions about companies connected to the looming peak oil crisis in the future.

Biofuels are created from recently dead biological materials such as corn oil or wood pulp. Still in its infancy, this approach produces nowhere near enough fuel to satisfy our needs. It's also more expensive to produce biofuel than it is to produce oil, so biofuel won't likely be economically attractive until oil prices rise considerably farther. What's more, the biofuel process results in the same kinds of pollution that petroleum refining produces. And finally, diverting resources from the production of food to produce energy could cause significant inflation in food prices.

Natural gas has been a choice favored by Boone Pickens. But natural gas is subject to its own supply limitations and the United States probably has already passed the point of "peak gas." Natural gas is also difficult to store and ship across oceans.

Hybrid cars driven by a combination of gasoline engines and electric motors have proven very popular, their fuel savings offsetting their often anemic performance. All-electric, plug-in automobiles are just coming to the market and seem, for the moment, to be the best solution to conserving petroleum because they use none, although the electricity to charge them may come from petroleum or coal-fired plants. The downside is that current battery technology can only provide about a forty-mile range, enough for city commuting but not enough to warrant replacing a gasoline car entirely.

Cheap oil fueled the growth of American suburbs and today, in the largest cities, some workers drive more than an hour to get to their jobs. As oil prices rise there is likely to be greater interest in mass transit, even in mid-sized cities. Over a longer period we may see the end of the suburbs and a return to city living. "Local" may become the new buzzword. You work where you live, you meet by teleconference rather than flying from one city to another, and you buy your produce from a local farmers market rather than from a major grocery chain. And the food you buy may be grown with "natural fertilizers" (that means manure) and not the petroleum-based fertilizers that have become so prevalent.

But don't think we're painting some idyllic pastoral picture here. There are tough consequences associated with the era of tough oil: inflation, turmoil in the Middle East, and competition, perhaps military, for the dwindling supplies of oil being produced. China already is moving aggressively to secure long-term supply contracts and to partner with Third World nations in a search for more oil reserves in remote parts of Africa.

Investment Opportunities in Oil

BP finally managed to halt the flow of oil into the Gulf of Mexico. Although the specific driller implicated in the spill is Transocean (RIG) the entire sector of drillers came under scrutiny from regulators and investors alike. The fear among investors was that there would be a permanent ban on drillers and oil refiners, especially those with exposure to the Gulf of Mexico. Wrong! The need for oil is going to override the concerns about deepwater drilling. If when you read this the prices of drillers are still below their pre-Gulf accident levels, fade the fear and add them to your portfolio.

Principle One: Fade the Fear

The major oil companies not implicated in the spill—Conoco-Phillips (COP), Chevron (CVX), and Exxon (XOM)—may also be attractively priced as fallout from the disaster. It may be especially interesting to look closely at Exxon, which is the largest company in the world with a market cap of $286 billion as of this writing. This company has survived multiple panics, crises, spills, and worries about gluts or droughts of oil. And along the way it has increased its dividend for twenty-eight consecutive years. Buying shares of companies with a history of steadily increasing dividends is, in and of itself, a very sound investment strategy in that companies raise dividends when they are confident of their future earnings potential.

Let's take a moment to look at the S&P Dividend Aristocrats Index, a list that Standard & Poor's compiles each year listing all companies that have increased dividends for twenty-five consecutive years. How has this index done overall? Is it better than simply buying an index of all stocks?

Absolutely! Since 1989 the Dividend Aristocrats have returned 12.93% annually, versus 11.8% for the S&P 500 as a whole. During the 2000–2002 bear market the Dividend Aristocrats returned 0% while the rest of the market collapsed in a severe downturn. In the five years ending in 2009, a period of immense volatility, the Dividend Aristocrats returned 3.32% versus 0.42% for the S&P 500.

Here is the current constituent list:

3M Co.	MMM	Integrys Energy Group Inc.	TEG
Abbott Laboratories	ABT	Johnson & Johnson	JNJ
AFLAC Inc.	AFL	Kimberly-Clark	KMB
Air Products & Chemicals Inc.	APD	Leggett & Platt	LEG
Archer-Daniels-Midland Co.	ADM	Lilly, Eli & Co.	LLY
Automatic Data Processing	ADP	Lowe's Cos. Inc.	LOW
Bard, C.R. Inc.	BCR	McDonald's Corp.	MCD
Becton, Dickinson & Co.	BDX	McGraw-Hill Cos. Inc.	MHP
Bemis Co. Inc.	BMS	PPG Industries Inc.	PPG
Brown-Forman Corp. B	BF/B	PepsiCo Inc.	PEP
Centurytel Inc.	CTL	Pitney Bowes Inc.	PBI
Chubb Corp.	CB	Procter & Gamble	PG
Cincinnati Financial Corp.	CINF	Questar Corp.	STR
Cintas Corp.	CTAS	Sherwin-Williams Co.	SHW
Clorox Co.	CLX	Sigma-Aldrich Corp.	SIAL
Coca-Cola Co.	KO	Stanley Black & Decker	SWK
Consolidated Edison Inc.	ED	Supervalu Inc.	SVU
Dover Corp.	DOV	Target Corp.	TGT
Emerson Electric Co.	EMR	VF Corp.	VFC
ExxonMobil Corp.	XOM	Walmart Stores	WMT
Family Dollar Stores Inc.	FDO	Walgreen Co.	WAG
Grainger, W.W. Inc.	GWW		

When applying our "Fade the Fear" principle during the occasional moments when media-inspired panic grips the markets, you can err on the side of safety by buying the companies that have solidly delivered rising dividends for more than a quarter of a century. While companies like Exxon fell more than 10% in the fears triggered by the Gulf oil spill, there is little question that the company will thrive again, with its stock price hitting new highs and its dividend rising yet again.

Outperformance of the Dividend Aristocrats over the S&P 500 from 1989 to 2008:

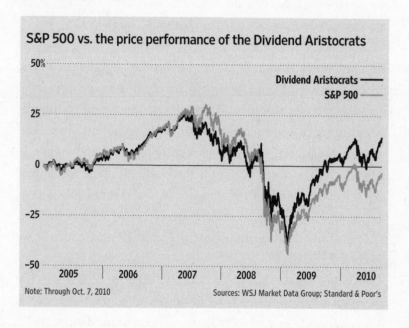

S&P 500 vs. the price performance of the Dividend Aristocrats

Note: Through Oct. 7, 2010

Sources: WSJ Market Data Group; Standard & Poor's

Principle Two: Invest through the Back Door

The back door for tough oil includes anything related to alternative energy, and the key with a back-door stock is to be certain that the front-door business is relatively safe and growing despite the fluctuations in the price of oil. As expected, most companies that are tied closely to alternative energy experience a lot of stock price volatility as oil prices rise and fall. Companies that are solely engaged in wind energy, solar energy, or natural gas might be in or out of business depending entirely on whether the price of oil stays above or below certain levels for an extended period of time. That's just too risky.

A great back-door example in the alternative energy space is Archer Daniel Midland (ADM). This is the largest agricultural processing company in the world, involved in everything from harvesting to the storage and transportation of food commodities ranging from vegetable oils to seeds, tofu, and corn. And where there is corn, there is a back door into alternative energy: ethanol. If oil prices rise, ADM stock will go up as companies depend increasingly on shipments of the ethanol ADM produces. If oil prices go down, no problem: ADM has been in business for a century and is among the dividend aristocrats we discussed earlier.

Another sector that holds potential back-door plays in the alternative energy space is wind power. One great example is AeroVironment, a company that has been around since 1971, has lots of cash and no debt, and generates a ton of cash from its primary business: making unmanned aircraft systems that hang out in the stratosphere spying on potential enemies, checking out hurricanes and forest fires, and carrying out other airborne tasks for its military and corporate customers. The company has been growing at 25% per year for the past several years. But what, you ask, does this company have to do with wind power? The company has used its knowledge of aerodynamics to create and patent miniature wind towers on top of buildings to help supply the buildings' energy demands. No big, expensive, land-grabbing wind farms required.

Otter Tail, a utility company that uses its excess cash flows to invest in other businesses (much as does Berkshire Hathaway), is another back-door play on wind energy. One of the businesses it invests in is DMI Industries, one of the largest makers of wind towers. It just opened new plants to meet rising demand. But no matter what happens to its wind power business, Otter Tail will always have its foundational utility business, which boasts Bill Gates as its second-largest shareholder, as well as a healthy dividend.

The Department of Energy estimates that wind power will account for 30% of our energy needs by 2030, up from just 3% today. That's a Nostradamus-style prediction, but if it is right there's going to be nonstop business for these two stocks. And if it's wrong, it doesn't matter, since you can essentially buy the wind businesses of these two companies for free given how well their main businesses are doing.

Principle Three: Invest through the Front Door

The front-door entries for tough oil are those companies we will rely on to get us the difficult-to-find oil as easy reserves dwindle. The spill that ravaged the Gulf of Mexico will not change the basic fact that most of the remaining oil in the world is to be found offshore. Exploiting these deposits will require specialized equipment and techniques very few companies possess. The three big gorillas of offshore drilling are Noble Corp. (NE), Diamond Offshore (DO), and Transocean (RIG). They usually have long-term contracts with the oil majors that provide some stability to their stock prices, and all three are expected to benefit long-term as our demand for oil increases while supplies become increasingly difficult to harvest.

FIVE

IS IT JUST ME, OR IS IT GETTING WARMER?

The Looming Threat of Global Warming

I T'S DIFFICULT TO BE neutral on the subject of global warming. There are political agendas, religious agendas, and financial agendas on both sides of the equation and often these agendas are even merged with one another.

You can decide where you stand along the spectrum from confirmed believer that manmade warming is occurring to dedicated denier, but, in the end, where you stand doesn't really matter. More than any other apocalyptic event we discuss in this book, global warming illustrates one of our central tenets: what you believe isn't important, it's what everyone else believes. And in this case many government leaders and the vast majority of climate scientists around the globe believe that global warming is real, that it's being caused in large measure by human economic activity, and that its consequences will be catastrophic on a global scale if the trend is not reversed.

Nevertheless, the debate continues with one side blaming human activity, the other arguing that warming may just be the result of the natural cycles of the Earth. But it is precisely this confusion and obsession about the environment and about climate change that creates opportunity for the investor. Money is going to be spent. Many governments have already begun to mandate all sorts of measures to reduce carbon emissions, and those mandates will expand exponentially as political pressure increases.

Whether you consider manmade global warming a legitimate concern or a mass delusion, it's critical at this point to protect your portfolio accordingly to take advantage of the popular direction that governments are going on this. Governments themselves and the companies that reside within their jurisdictions will spend many hundreds of billions of dollars over the next twenty years to reduce emissions and attempt to counter the effects of carbon already in the atmosphere. New technologies will emerge, as will new financial markets for things like "cap and trade," one of the more likely mechanisms for providing incentives and punishments for carbon emitters.

The Roots of the Global Warming Crisis

For all of the fraught arguments back and forth about global warming, the science that underlies it is pretty simple. It begins with the sun radiating massive amounts of energy into space. A tiny portion of that energy comes through the Earth's atmosphere and is absorbed by the ground and surface water. Those "hot" surfaces then reradiate heat into the atmosphere at different wavelengths than sunlight. If Earth did not have an atmosphere, virtually all of that reradiated energy would be lost into space (and we wouldn't be here to argue about warming, since there would be no oxygen and the Earth would be a much colder place). But our atmosphere, composed mostly of nitrogen and life-giving oxygen with traces of other gases and water vapor, acts as a blanket, absorbing some of the reradiated energy and warming enough to provide us with a relatively large comfort zone between the two poles.

It is the content of the atmosphere—how much of the various gases it contains—that becomes the issue at hand. While the main components of the atmosphere do not absorb much of the reradiated energy from the Earth's surface, other gases do. Their capacity to absorb this heat gives them their collective name: greenhouse gases. Some of them occur naturally, some are the combined product of nature and human activity, and some are solely created by human beings. The principle greenhouse gases are carbon dioxide, methane, and nitrous oxide. Other significant greenhouse gases produced almost exclusively by industrial sources are hydrofluorocarbons, perfluorocarbons, and sulfur hexafluoride. Put simply, all other things being equal, the more greenhouse gases in the atmosphere, the warmer the atmosphere becomes. And there is no doubt that the amount of greenhouse gases in the atmosphere is increasing and has been for more than a century. Worse, the rate of increase is increasing.

Going Green

The fear of global climate change is at least somewhat related to the problem of oil, which, as we explained in the previous chapter, is becoming increasingly difficult to find and extract. In this chapter, we'll look at two strategies that are being employed to help solve the problems caused by the burning of fossil fuels—strategies that tie closely to the investment opportunities surrounding global warming.

Strategy One: Develop alternative energy technologies to replace coal and oil.

Most of us are familiar with the two most popularly discussed alternative energy sources right now, namely wind and solar. Big windmills and solar panels are the products that capture "free" energy from the sun and the wind and most large utilities in the United States are using those methods to produce at least a small portion of their power output. But there are also old standbys. Hydropower from dams is one, albeit one that is falling out of favor given the growing problems attached to fresh water supplies. Nuclear power is another. Following the tragic meltdown of the Chernobyl power plant in 1986, however, nuclear power has been growing only slowly, and it certainly isn't something the green movement endorses. Nonetheless, it is one of the few sources of power that could conceivably produce enough power to eliminate most coal and oil-fired power plants. Finally, while there are many other potential sources of energy, we are only beginning to understand their potential. Some of these options include geothermal power, power generated by tides and ocean currents, and power derived from the methane produced by rotting garbage.

Strategy Two: Increase energy efficiency to reduce oil consumption.

Many people believe that alternative methods of generating power are a crucial first step toward avoiding global warming related catastrophes, but they are only part of the solution. The other part is becoming more efficient, that is, consuming less power. If we can slow the growth of power demand we can build fewer power plants and burn less fossil fuel in the future. And the opportunities to do that are remarkable, beginning with the popularity of automobiles like Toyota's innovative Prius hybrid. Other similar cars, including all-electric vehicles that plug into an outlet to recharge their batteries, are coming to market. Appliances are becoming more efficient and many of us will be reading from the light generated by highly efficient light emitting diodes in the next few years.

Much more can also be done with energy infrastructure. The big high-tension wires that carry power from generating plants to communities and factories far away could be much more efficient, for example. Wires formed of new materials could prevent much of the "leakage" that now occurs in long-distance transmission, in effect increasing the capacity of a generating plant without burning more fuel. Computerized controls, both on the electrical grid itself and inside our homes, will be able to monitor power demand and better coordinate supply. We'll be recharging our electric cars at night when overall demand for electricity is lower, thus getting more efficient utilization of capital-intensive power stations. And during the day, when electrical demand surges, the power company will be able to tap the batteries of hundreds of thousands of electric vehicles to prevent brownouts and blackouts.

Both of these strategies offer significant opportunites for companies that create products or services that help to reduce greenhouse gas emissions. Let's take a closer look at the myriad investment implications of global warming.

Investing Implications of Global Warming

In terms of global warming, the fear is ongoing. There is no fade the fear. Either the Earth is warming because of human activity, or it isn't. What matters is that people are obsessed with "climate change" and they always will be, and, because of our global prosperity over the past century, we have the luxury to explore other technologies and alternative fuels to help power our society. So let's look at some of the safest and most effective ways at creating alternative energy. In this case it makes more sense to explore the options by their general categories.

Alternative Energy Plays

Given the human propensity to always find something to worry about, global warming tends to come to the fore mostly when everything else is going well, the economy is booming, and people are feeling good about their lives. So what if we have our two cars and our nice house, our kids are healthy, and our neighbors are friendly? Evidence of this tendency can be found in Google Trends, which tracks how many instances of a particular search phrase are occurring over time. Typing in the phrase "global warming" shows how often people are searching for that phrase on Google. It's a barometer of our fear of climate change.

The chart shows queries—proxies for fear or concern—about "global warming" peaking in early 2007 just as the economy and the stock market were peaking, too. In other words, when everything else was going well in our lives, we were worried about climate change. And when did worries about "global warming" hit a multi-year low? The market crash in 2008 coincides very closely to a huge drop in queries about "global warming" and

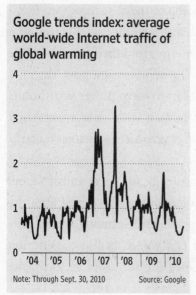

Google trends index: average world-wide Internet traffic of global warming

Note: Through Sept. 30, 2010   Source: Google

they fell even farther as unemployment rose. When we had a real here-and-now problem to worry about, global climate change took a back seat.

One of the people we most respect for sheer intellectual fire-power is a professor at a major university. He posed to us this question: we don't know if global warming is true or not, but what if there is just a 1% chance that it is true and not only that, but that the effects are exponential, that once global warming begins to create real problems they begin to cascade swiftly and cataclysmically? Shouldn't we err on the side of defending against its effects rather than simply ignoring it, even if there's only a one-in-a-hundred chance it could happen?

What does this mean for investors?

First, panicked attempts to find alternative energies that require government subsidies to make them succeed are long-term losers. Take the solar industry. As noble as it is to find a source of power that draws its energy from the ultimate source of power, solar power simply isn't workable right now. The only way in which it is currently cost-effective to power your home, or any other building for that matter, with solar energy is if there is no cap to the amount of government subsidies a country provides.

Spain tried to do a no-cap subsidy for solar and it failed. Costs were simply too great. Solar revenues dropped 80% the year after it removed the no-cap subsidy. Germany, which generates lots of revenues for solar companies, is also considering dropping its no-cap subsidy. Once the subsidies go away, the industry will go away.

The second alternative power source that generates a lot of attention (and some government subsidies) is the wind, which is an indirect form of solar energy (the sun's energy generates atmospheric temperature and pressure discrepancies that in turn generate wind). Interest in wind power waxes and wanes, gaining a lot of media attention when well-known investors get involved. Back in 2007 T. Boone Pickens was on CNBC and in *The Wall Street Journal* and the *New York Times*, trashing America's dependence on foreign oil and touting the benefits of wind power. As we mentioned in the last chapter, the Department of Energy estimates that wind power is going to go from generating 3% of our energy needs to about 30% by the year 2030. If that is correct—and we don't trust any forecast that looks that far into the future—then wind power stocks should get a big lift. And if it's wrong, it doesn't matter. By taking the back-door approach to investing in wind energy, we can find companies whose primary businesses are doing so well that their small investments in wind energy basically give us a free play on wind. Here are two back-door plays: the same two plays mentioned earlier, AeroVironment (AVAV) and Otter Tail (OTTR), work as excellent back-door plays here. What we like about them is that they are both under the radar, not broadly followed by Wall Street (despite one of the richest men in the world, Bill Gates, being the largest investor in Otter Tail), and will grow quickly with interest in wind power. Of the major alternative energy sources, the one that holds the most promise is nuclear power. We know this, in part, because it is already in use around the world. We also already all know the problems with nuclear energy: it is relatively expensive to build nuclear power plants; if things go wrong they can go disastrously wrong; and we don't know the solution to disposing of nuclear waste. But those concerns begin to pale when we consider the benefits of nuclear power:

- Zero emissions.

- Cheaper than solar, wind, oil, even natural gas.

- The technology has become significantly safer as operating experience accumulates in places like France, which produces more than 80% of its energy through nuclear power generation.

So nuclear power certainly takes the lead among alternative power sources and that gives investors a potential path to profits with stocks like these:

Cameco (CCJ) is a clear front-door play on nuclear power because it is the world's largest uranium producer, accounting for around 19% of world production. The company has a joint venture with GE in which CCJ supplies uranium that GE will enrich for power use. And it doesn't hurt that Cameco also mines gold.

American Ecology (ECOL) is the back-door play into nuclear energy. Forget about all the politics involving whether or not we should build new nuclear reactors. This company is the perfect play on cleaning up the waste that's generated by the reactors we currently have. It has virtually no competition and probably won't because of the huge costs and technological expertise to start a company that cleans up nuclear waste at power plants. It's also in the business of recycling oil waste, making it a potential play on increasing oil prices. It's eco-friendly, solves a major problem, and you can be a total global warming agnostic or atheist and still make money.

Emissions Plays

Regardless of the debate about whether human emissions are driving global warming, it is worth having at least some stocks that are focused on reducing emissions. These stocks should rise over time not just because of concerns about global warming, but also because pollution control is something that has been remarkably successful and much favored by populations in the industrialized or industrializing countries of the world. Emissions reduction has been so successful, in fact, that according to the Environmental Protection Agency (EPA), emissions caused by cars are one-fourth of what they were in 1970, the year the agency was founded. If we concentrate on automotive emissions technology, we come up with three plays.

Borg-Warner (BWA) makes automotive systems. Up to 70% of company sales are derived from technologies and applications that increase fuel efficiency and/or reduce emissions. Magna International (MGA) also makes complete automotive systems that it then sells to the major car companies. The company's hydroforming business is a key technology in creating lighter and stronger cars. Finally, OM Group (OMG) owns thirteen thousand tons of cobalt, a crucial element for manufacturing batteries to power the coming generation of hybrid automobiles. All three companies have strong traditional businesses that will continue to generate cash flows regardless of our worries on global warming. And yet an ever increasing part of that cash flow will be driven by the need to make lighter, more fuel-efficient vehicles with cleaner emissions.

Efficiency Plays

The problem with energy consumption, pollution, emissions, and global warming isn't always the companies, though. Sometimes it's the customers. We consume oil, we consume gas, we use and waste energy on a daily basis. During the oil spill in the Gulf people were eager to boycott BP service stations. Few were saying "let's turn the air conditioning down at night so we use energy more efficiently and hence have less need for oil and gas." Instead we just kept driving and turning on the air conditioning to stay comfortable.

But there are technologies to enable us to use energy more efficiently. One is called the "smart grid," a method and technology by which energy is distributed through the utility system according to who needs the energy the most. Most electric grids right now are dumb; electricity is sent out and anyone who wants can tap into it. However, by using sophisticated routing technology we can determine the biggest consumers of electricity and make sure that more electricity is sent to those consumers than to those who are not the biggest users. As usual, there are front-door ways and back-door ways to play smart grid technology.

Cisco (CSCO) is a back-door opportunity known for its Internet routing technologies. They make sure the bits and bytes that go through the Internet end up at the right locations in the fastest amount of time. When a single byte leaves your computer on its way to another one around the world, Cisco routers are usually involved in making sure those bytes get there safely and quickly. Cisco has $40 billon cash in the bank and is obviously unlikely to go out of business with over $10 billion a year in earnings before interest and taxes.

With its experience routing through networks like the Internet, it's no surprise that Cisco is tiptoeing into the (potentially) multi-hundred-billion-dollar smart grid market with the recent purchase of GridNet, a San Francisco–based company.

Another back-door play is Intel. With the entire electric utility grid going to smart technologies, chips will be needed, and Intel is the biggest chip maker in the world. With $16 billion cash in the bank and cash flow of $14 billion as we write this book, Intel can scale up quickly with the smart grid industry.

The front-door companies are companies that are already profitable, already have the bulk of their revenues in the space, and are growing with the sector. They include Echelon Corporation (ELON), Itron (ITRI), and Comverge (COMV).

All three companies provide the parts, components, and services to build out the smart grid infrastructure. All three companies have 100% of their revenues devoted to the sector, are growing, and have cash in the bank.

Of course the problem that contributes to many of the issues of this book—peak oil, global warming, carbon emissions—is the fact that we all drive cars all the time. You can't really get people to stop driving cars and consuming oil, and, certainly, there have been advances that take that reality into account. For example, according to Matt Ridley, author of *The Rational Optimist,* a parked car in the United States in 1970 actually had more carbon emissions than a car today driving on the highway due to the leaks and other inefficiencies in cars forty years ago.

However, the real solution is the electric car. The problem, though, with making the electric car more practical and afford-able has always been the battery. Think of your laptop. You charge it all night. Then you take it on an airplane to watch a movie, and two hours into the movie the battery dies. How many batteries like that would it take to drive a car sixty miles an hour for ten hours?

The back door on the electric car companies is, of course, the major car companies. Ford, Toyota, and Honda are all involved in some form of electric car production, but it is only a small part of their business. Tesla (TSLA), a car company that focuses exclusively on electric cars, is developing an electric car for Toyota.

A better approach is to look at the battery companies. A123 Systems (AONE) makes rechargeable lithium-ion batteries and battery systems, both for both hybrid and pure electric passenger vehicles. China BAK Battery (CBAK) makes lithium-ion rechargeable batteries intended for use in light electric vehicles and other hybrids. Ener1 (HEV) also makes rechargeable lithium-ion batteries and battery systems. Its batteries are being used in hybrid, plug-in hybrid, and electric vehicles, busses, and trucks.

Between nuclear energy, anti-emissions technology, wind power, rechargeable batteries, and smart grid stocks, we feel this is a portfolio that counteracts the fears of global warming, while having the added side benefit of helping the world.

SIX

NOTHING TO FEAR
BUT FEAR ITSELF

The Threat of Terrorism

A DECADE AFTER THE EVENT certain words, names, and numbers still resonate with horror: 9/11, Twin Towers, Osama bin Laden, Muhammad Atta.

The attacks on the World Trade Center and the Pentagon are seared into our collective memory as the embodiment of terror. And among the apocalyptic events we consider in this book, terrorism remains our nation's greatest fear. A collision with an asteroid seems too remote a possibility; global warming is occurring at a glacial (excuse the pun) pace; and future shortages of fresh water and oil have not yet come into focus for most of us. Most people believe it is only a question of when, not if, there will be another terrorist attack, or, indeed, many more.

One reason we fear another terrorist attack, of course, is that the success of the 9/11 attacks sent such a powerful message to would-be jihadists. It took only nineteen young men armed with cheap box cutters to kill three thousand people, turn the world's most iconic buildings into burning heaps of rubble, and strike at the heart of the world's mightiest military machine. The attacks prompted two hugely expensive and deadly wars in the Middle East and have cost the United States untold billions in lost productivity and government spending on homeland security. The attacks will go down in history as the ultimate example of asymmetric warfare, a struggle waged between a huge and technologically sophisticated military and a primitive, poorly-armed band of irregulars.

Another reason we fear terrorism is that we don't know what form it will take. As is often stated, the terrorists have to succeed only once while we must never fail in our vigilance. But where do we watch and what do we watch for? The next attack may come in the form of anthrax spores dumped out of a plastic baggie on a windy day from the observation platform atop the Empire State Building. Or perhaps Chicago's water supply will be poisoned with a deadly chemical. A dirty bomb—a conventional explosive surrounded by radioactive material that will be scatted by the explosion—may go off in downtown Atlanta. Or it may be the threat we fear most: terrorists smuggle a full-fledged atomic bomb into the country in a shipping container and detonate it by remote control as the container moves through Los Angeles. When, where, and how to strike is entirely in the hands of the terrorists. No wonder we're scared.

But as we consider various other apocalyptic events—destruction by an asteroid or climate change that profoundly alters the global environment—we need to put terrorism in its proper perspective. We doubtless will offend many people who will deem us uncaring or unpatriotic, but the fact of the matter is that the number of people who died in the 9/11 attacks is about the average number of Americans who die every month on our highways. And yes, defending against further attacks is a costly burden, but the cost pales beside the financial havoc wrought here and around the globe by our biggest banks and their risky bets using complex financial instruments they didn't understand.

And it wasn't as if we hadn't been warned. Islamic fanatics had already detonated a bomb in the basement of the World Trade Center eight years earlier and government was explicitly warned about terrorists using airliners against us just a month before the actual attacks. Finally, it isn't just evildoers from abroad we need to worry about. Prior to the 9/11 attacks, the worst terrorist experience we had endured was at the hands of a U.S. Army veteran espousing his love and devotion to the United States Constitution. On April 19, 1995, Timothy McVeigh killed 168 people, including women and children, when he set off an explosion that tore off the front of the Alfred P. Murrah Federal Building in Oklahoma City.

As we will see in the following discussion of the various terrorist scenarios that might play out tomorrow or ten years from tomorrow, terrorism probably is the least apocalyptic of the things we need to worry about. Yet while terrorist acts aren't likely to be either pervasive or persistent, our *fear* of terrorism is both pervasive and persistent. In that disconnect lies opportunity.

Nuclear Terrorism

A nuclear weapon exploding in the middle of Manhattan or Washington, D.C., certainly is the terrorists' fondest dream and our worst fear. And rightly so. The effects of a nuclear explosion are almost too fantastic to be believed. Unlike conventional explosives that generate temperatures at the blast site of a few thousand degrees, the immense energy liberated by even a small amount of enriched uranium or plutonium produces temperatures of a million degrees or more in the core of the blast. As the blast front expands it vaporizes everything in the immediate vicinity, including steel and concrete. While the temperature quickly drops as the blast front expands, the powerful shock wave generated in the explosion levels buildings and kills all life. At the same time the explosion spews deadly radiation, perhaps the most terrifying aspect of the explosion. The initial radiation is in the form of neutrons and gamma rays followed by residual radiation from vaporized material that cools and condenses into particles in the atmosphere and returns to earth as radioactive fallout. Some of those particles can be carried a hundred miles or more downwind to contaminate a large swath of ground. The good news is that, unlike an airburst a thousand or more feet above the ground that spreads destruction widely, a terrorist bomb would almost certainly be detonated at ground level. But while the blast effects would be much less than an airburst, the fallout generated by the cratering effect of a ground blast would be much worse. The casualties in such an attack could well total nearly a million dead and more than a million injured by flying debris, falling buildings, direct burns, and radiation and radioactive fallout.

Needless to say the collateral damage of such an attack would continue for years. If New York was the target the city's role as a global financial center would end. If Washington was in the terrorists' crosshairs, the national government could become essentially helpless, "decapitated" in the language of nuclear war planners. The impact of such an event on our national psyche and our economy is inestimable.

Could it happen? Perhaps. But it is easy to underestimate the difficulty of building a nuclear weapon. To the best of our knowledge only a handful of nations have had the money and the technology to put together a bomb and it is inconceivable that a group of terrorists hiding in caves could even begin to understand where to start. It is not so inconceivable, however, that terrorists could find someone, somewhere to sell them a small nuclear weapon, perhaps a tactical warhead used on a small missile or in a torpedo. We know that Russia has done very poorly in tracking and securing its own arsenal of nuclear weapons since the Soviet Union broke apart. "Loose nukes" from Russia are the most likely source of a weapon for terrorists. While Pakistan and North Korea can both be regarded as nuclear rogues that might one day be tempted to visit some form of revenge on the United States, their arsenals are likely to remain extremely small for years to come.

Given the difficulty of building or obtaining a nuclear weapon, many terrorism experts theorize that the next best option for determined terrorists is a "dirty" bomb. Such a weapon would consist of a conventional explosive surrounded by radioactive material. The resulting explosion would not produce anything like the blast and thermal effects of a nuclear weapon but it would hurl pieces of radioactive debris over a wide area, the dimensions of which would be determined by the size of the conventional blast. From the terrorists' standpoint the value of such a weapon is that it seizes on our fear of radioactivity. In effect, the radioactive debris acts as a "force multiplier" that makes a conventional explosion much more frightening.

The problem confronting the terrorists trying to assemble a dirty bomb is that any radioactive material that is "hot" enough to be terrifying is very dangerous to handle. The most likely victims of any such bomb will be the terrorists who die from radiation poisoning while assembling or transporting it. Still, we have ample evidence that some terrorists will gladly give their lives to hurt and humble their enemy. So we would have to rank this threat as more plausible than a nuclear bomb, but still highly unlikely. And even if it occurred the damage would be orders of magnitude lower than that produced by a nuclear explosion.

The catastrophic explosion and meltdown of the Chernobyl power plant in April 1986 is ample evidence that a nuclear catastrophe can occur without a weapon. The number of dead and injured and of those who have or will develop cancer or other radiation-related diseases isn't known, but the extent of the disaster is clear and raises the question of how much damage terrorists could inflict on us by sabotaging a nuclear power plant or flying into it with an airliner as they did the Twin Towers and the Pentagon. The answer is probably not much. While no structure as complicated as a nuclear power plant is 100% fail-safe, the far more extensive safety systems in U.S. power plants compared to those in Russian plants make it extremely unlikely that internal sabotage could cause a Chernobyl-type meltdown. And the thick steel-reinforced containment buildings that house the reactor cores could probably withstand a direct hit from even a large passenger aircraft. Even in the unlikely event that the containment building was breached, the radioactivity released would probably be minimal. Nearby residents would be plenty scared, but most likely would suffer no ill consequences.

Bioterrorism

No one has effectively explained the source and motivation behind the spurt of letters containing anthrax spores sent to U.S. news organizations and to two Democratic senators just weeks after the 9/11 attacks. The anthrax caused outbreaks of the disease in at least twenty-two people and killed five. The initial speculation tried to focus blame on al-Qaeda or Iraq, but the investigation turned fairly quickly to domestic sources. Yet it wasn't until 2008 that the FBI identified Dr. Bruce Ivins, a biodefense researcher at Ft. Detrick in Maryland, as a primary suspect. Ivins soon after committed suicide and was never charged with or indicted in the anthrax letters.

But the anthrax letters were not the first bioterrorism attack on the United States. In 1984 members of a cult called Rajneeshee spread salmonella on the offerings at a pizza parlor's salad bar and poured the bacteria into salad dressing and other menu items at other local restaurants in The Dalles, Oregon. No one died, but more than seven hundred people got sick, some seriously so. The motivation: to incapacitate enough voters that the cult could vote itself into control of the county government.

Bioterrorism is scary because it can be carried out with great stealth and the consequences of some of the diseases are truly horrific: anthrax destroys the lungs, bubonic plague causes extreme pain as it kills the skin while the victim is still alive and the various hemorrhagic fevers, such as Marburg and Ebola, cause massive and uncontrolled bleeding from virtually every orifice. It takes days after exposure for symptoms to emerge. An anthrax attack, for instance, might first be evidenced by an unusually large number of people visiting hospital emergency rooms with breathing difficulties similar to a bad case of flu. Only after one person dies and pathologists examine a culture would anthrax be diagnosed. Many of the initial wave of patients would be fatally ill by that point. As word spread of the cause of the growing death toll, a panicked population could easily overwhelm medical facilities demanding treatment even though they wouldn't know if they had been exposed to the pathogen. If the attack was successful from the standpoint of the terrorists, all available medical facilities within a hundred miles of the attack may be called upon to provide beds and treatment. The initially high death toll would quickly wane as sick people got necessary treatment, but even when treated inhalation anthrax is fatal to half of those suffering. Hundreds or even thousands of people could die, depending upon the method used to distribute the anthrax spores. Still, the damage would be contained to a relatively small geographic area *unless* the terrorists were well organized and planned carefully to conduct simultaneous attacks on a dozen or more large cities.

How worried should we be about such an attack? Certainly there are sources of anthrax spores and other pathogens available on global black markets. The Soviet Union experimented extensively with methods to "weaponize" anthrax and has been less than candid about the results and what has become of the stockpiles and scientists who conducted those experiments. We shudder to think about the human consequences of a terrorist perched on the Observation Deck of the Empire State Building emptying a purse full of anthrax spores into the air. It could happen. Less likely, though, is a well-coordinated attack in many cities. Few cities have a population as concentrated as midtown Manhattan, so the total number of people exposed in other cities would be much less and perhaps not seen as tempting targets.

Cyberterrorism

Information is the lifeblood of any modern economy and none more so than the information-addicted U.S. economy. We may have a second-class broadband market compared to some European and Asian countries, but vast amounts of information flow through those old copper conduits. We are highly dependent upon the Internet for critical financial data and transactions, military information, and even the operation of such critical structures as power plants, the electricity grid, water systems, and dams. If you're personally addicted to the Web you know how frustrating an unexpected interruption of service can be. And so do terrorists.

Individually we worry about having our financial data or other personal information residing on our computer "hacked" and our security software occasionally alerts us to a potential threat. But that's nothing compared to the nearly continuous probing conducted against the Defense Department's computers from foreign sources, whether individual hackers or government intelligence agents. The same is doubtless true of other government agencies, such as the Federal Reserve and the Federal Aviation Administration. Our big banks and utility companies have been probed and have had data stolen and even companies as technologically sophisticated as Google have been hacked. You may be one of the hundreds of thousands of Americans who have suffered the frustration and expense of identity theft. But with the exception of the frequent and irritating interruptions to service from our less-than-totally-reliable Internet service providers, the information networks have operated as intended.

But what if terrorists could shut down our electrical grid, turn off the FAA's air traffic control system, or sabotage a big bank's financial and trading data? The consequences of any of those actions could be severe and expensive. If a terrorist organization could find a way to sabotage the electrical grid, for example, a large part of the country might go dark for a while. Things like ATMs, traffic lights, and home appliances would shut down, although after the Y2K scare in the late 1990s most facilities that cannot afford to be without power—hospitals, factories, and large business headquarters, for example—have emergency generators. It probably wouldn't take utilities long to figure out the problem and restore power, so for the most part such an attack would be a massive and expensive inconvenience. The failure of the FAA's air traffic control system would be even less consequential. Pilots would still have their navigational and flight instruments and could talk to one another and to air traffic controllers over radios. Planes might be diverted from busy airports like Kennedy, O'Hare, or Atlanta to less congested areas to reduce the chances of a midair collision, and hundreds of thousands of travelers would be irritated at being stranded far from home. Again, a massive and expensive inconvenience.

An attack on a major U.S. bank or even on the Federal Reserve system is another matter. Recall that it was the failure of Lehman Brothers, a large—but far from the largest—financial services firm, that became one of the triggers of the global financial crisis in 2008. Firms like Lehman, Citigroup, and J.P. Morgan, along with large financial institutions in other countries, had a highly complex set of relationships with one another that depended upon vast amounts of information about each firm's financial condition. When Lehman failed all those banks began to wonder who among them might be next. Fearing that they might be caught holding the bag if another firm went down, they tried to call in their obligations and quit making new deals. Liquidity, the ease with which money flows back and forth from lender to borrower, dried up and dragged down businesses of every sort that depended on their ability to tap financial markets. Should a terrorist group manage to cripple one or more big banks it could trigger a similar crisis of confidence that could, in turn, lead to another global recession.

How likely are any of these cyber scenarios? Not very. Experts think it would take an extremely powerful computer system and very detailed knowledge of the workings of the institutions targeted for the attack. Hacking is one thing, bringing down a networked system like the U.S. electric grid is several orders of magnitude more difficult. But it is not impossible. In 2010 a Chinese graduate engineering student, Wang Jianwei, found himself under attack before the House Foreign Affairs Committee for having written an article entitled "Cascade-Based Attack Vulnerability on the U.S. Power Grid" in the international journal *Safety Science*. The article, he explained, was not intended to foment an attack on the U.S. power grid, but to explore its vulnerabilities with an eye toward enhancing the stability of the grid. Some remain suspicious. Wang's knowledge of how the U.S. power grid is interlinked was very sophis-ticated and could be used to cripple the grid. But experts in the field defended his research as a legitimate and useful topic to protect large networks such as the power grid.

We should never underestimate the ingenuity of people and organizations that would do us harm. But as we have seen in these discussions of possible terrorist scenarios, neither should we overestimate the damage they can do. Deadly, expensive, and frightening? No doubt. Apocalyptic in scope? Almost cer-tainly not.

Investing Implications of Terrorism

When one is in the middle of a terrorist attack it feels like the end of the world. At the time of the 9/11 attacks James lived about three blocks from the World Trade Center. He was a day trader at the time, so he also worked from home. With his trad-ing partner Dan, he had just finished breakfast right at the bottom of the towers and was walking back to the home office. Dan said, "Is the president coming to the city today?" And they looked up in the air because heading right at them, just six hundred feet up, was a plane they figured was Air Force One. Then, seconds later, the aircraft plunged directly into the World Trade Center. It certainly felt like the end of the world then, not only to James and Dan sitting there at ground zero, but to all of the families involved and then the millions of investors and traders who in panic sold the U.S. and global markets when the U.S. market reopened a week later on September 17. But this chart, which begins at September 1, shows the dips into September 21 and then the subsequent recovery to a post-9/11 high less than a year later.

Another example is the date now known as "7/7," the date in 2005 when Islamic terrorists staged a coordinated attack on the London rail system, setting off strategically placed bombs that killed fifty-two people and injured seven hundred.

The U.S. markets opened significantly down at 1184. The market then reversed, closing at the high of the day, 1198, which was higher than the close the day before. The market then went up the next four days in a row, reaching a high of 1223 over the next week. Obviously the markets were not applauding the news of terrorism but rather concluding that yes, terrorism occurred, but the world economy continues almost undeterred.

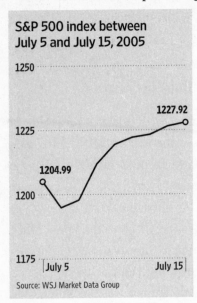

S&P 500 index between July 5 and July 15, 2005

1250

1227.92

1225

1204.99

1200

1175

July 5   July 15

Source: WSJ Market Data Group

Principle One: Fade the Fear

This rule will apply every time (with a caveat, of course, but hold that thought until the end of the chapter). In the event of another terrorist attack, use a portion of your portfolio to buy or average into a broad-based index. Hold until the market is higher than it was the day before the terrorist attack occurred. People will still shop at the world's most popular store, Walmart, they will eat at the world's most popular restaurant, McDonalds, they will still use Google for news and ads, and they will still buy books at the world's most popular bookstore, Amazon.

It's also worth keeping in mind that behavioral economics has long taught us that the pains of losses far outlive and outshine the pleasures of gains. While terrorism is horrible and the pain felt as a result lasts for many years, the fact remains that the market tends to be ultimately unsympathetic to those who survive. Those who do not adjust their investments accordingly will find that the pain of their loss will not only include other people, but also their financial security. In the end, there's one simple rule to keep in mind: the market dips, then it recovers. In other words, if the world doesn't end, then you must be a buyer. How much should you buy? This question goes beyond general principles and depends on you as an individual. But here are some guidelines:

- Never use leverage buying these dips. September 17, 2001, through September 21, 2001, would've wiped you out, for instance.

- Put one-third of your eventual position size on the line at a time. This gives you three days to ease into the trade.

- Save plenty of gunpowder for the next set of general principles.

Principle Two: Invest through the Back Door

The back-door approach to terrorism is focused on companies that are solid, probably large-cap companies with good fundamentals in a variety of economic sectors that happen to also have divisions that will do well in the fight against terrorism.

The classic example is General Electric (GE). GE will undoubtedly dip in any true market panic, but the company bought its way into the antiterror business when it bought a previously front-door company, Invision, which makes the scanners that many airports use to scan luggage going through security.

Tyco (TYC) is another example of a broadly diversified conglomerate that makes products ranging from coat hangers to fire extinguishers. It also makes security systems, ranging from video detection systems to intrusion detection systems.

Lockheed-Martin (LMT) makes fighter jets, tactical missiles, unmanned reconnaissance aircraft, rockets for the U.S. space program, and security systems for the Department of Defense. While this company would appear at first glance to be a front-door play (it's directly related to the problems that arise when terrorism occurs), as one of the leading defense contractors its services are needed both in wartime and peacetime. It also tends to be a solid bet throughout its history as can be seen in the chart on the opposite page:

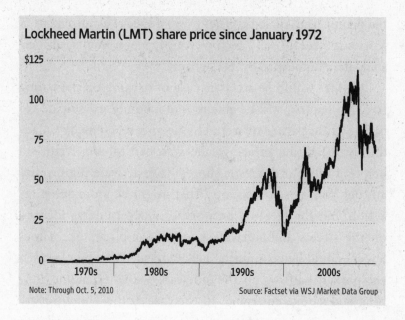

Lockheed Martin (LMT) share price since January 1972

Note: Through Oct. 5, 2010   Source: Factset via WSJ Market Data Group

Principle Three: Invest through the Front Door

Entire industries have sprung up around the quest to fight terrorism. Many of these companies are speculative and are still in
the process of developing and testing their technologies. That
said, owning a basket of the speculative companies that are
committed to fighting the more likely terrorism scenarios will
pay off in dividends.

In the wake of the Times Square bomb scare of May 2010,
the initial market reaction was to buy bomb detection stocks
such as Analogic (ALOG), which builds the scanners that are
used to analyze checked luggage at airports (as opposed to the
Invision scanners, which scan the luggage you are bringing on

the plane). The Analogic system uses a special arrangement of X-rays to peer at every inch of your luggage, leaving no personal item untouched by its electronic eyes.

But that would be a classic case of barking up the wrong tree. No scanner will be able to find a bomb in a suicide vehicle or a car parked on a street. The only real remedy (in addition to fighting the ringleaders abroad to stop terrorism before it hits our domestic shores) is to activate Big Brother and let him loose on society. That might be an extreme reaction, but the fact is a network of video cameras focused on the streets and sidewalks in popular places like Times Square could detect unusual behavior, such as a bomb-laden car parked halfway on the sidewalk with the engine running and smoke emerging. In the case of the Times Square bomb, vigilant bystanders saw exactly that and reported it to authorities.

We also need to prevent terrorists based here from getting funding from abroad. How do we do this? Terrorists don't do the same kinds of financial transactions that the rest of us do. Putting systems in place to track all of our banking transactions and look for unusual behavior is one step. The list of Big Brother possibilities goes on and on.

Fortunately, many of these technologies are not just speculative or experimental but are in place and already watching us and all of our activities in hopes of finding that one instance of bad behavior whose early detection can result in saved lives.

In the United States there are more than thirty million closed-circuit video cameras. If you live in a city, chances are your image is being captured, analyzed, and stored on more than four hundred different occasions throughout a single day. All of your bank and ATM transactions are analyzed. All of your instant messaging and website usage at your job is stored and potentially analyzed for misuse and then reported to managers. Your home is photographed from the sky every day. If you move suspiciously in a crowd, Big Brother will instantly notice.

Roughly $200 billion is spent annually in the United States on surveillance and monitoring. Human beings can't do it. A human being looking at a surveillance camera for more than twenty minutes routinely misses 95% of the activity that he's supposed to be catching. An entire industry has sprung up in the automation of this monitoring. These companies will continue to grow in a world that seems to be less safe each year.

Here are a few of the public companies that will benefit now and in years to come:

NICE systems (NICE): Started by seven ex–Israeli army soldiers, NICE has security productions ranging from motion detection in videos of crowds to detect unusual behavior within seconds, to monitoring bank transactions in search of automatically detecting fraud.

Analogic (ALOG): As we discussed earlier, when you check a bag at an airport, chances are it's going to go through a 3D X-ray scanner developed by Analogic. Any suspicious bags will be thoroughly photographed and tagged for an operator to examine further.

China Security & Surveillance (CSR): This company sells automated surveillance systems all over China to monitor everything from ports to sports stadiums to government buildings. Its earnings growth has been phenomenal and the stock price very appealing.

VeriSign (VRSN): Most people know VeriSign as the monopoly on domain-name registration. But one of its products keeps track of all of your ATM usage. If there's unusual activity (if someone is holding you at gunpoint and forcing you to withdraw money, for instance) VeriSign alerts the appropriate authorities.

Websense (WBSN): Approximately 50% of S&P 500 companies monitor their employees' Internet usage and e-mail usage. Websense offers products that do everything from Web filtering (so you can't spend too much time, if any, on shopping, betting, or porn sites, for instance) to actual e-mail monitoring (it can track if you are sending internal secrets or using e-mail too much for personal use). Over forty-two million employees are monitored by their employers using Websense software.

ArcSight (ARST): ArcSight keeps track of every keystroke logged in a corporate enterprise and examines the data for anything suspicious (such as the same user logging in at the same time from two different places). With everyone worried about the threat of cyberterrorism, ArcSight's profits have been soaring on solid sales gains.

DigitalGlobe (DGI): Every piece of the planet is imaged each day by DigitalGlobe cameras orbiting in satellites. Think Google Earth, but for the military. The company was formerly called "EarthWatch" but before going public changed its name to "DigitalGlobe."

GeoEye (GEOY): GeoEye is the only other company in the satellite imaging space and is known for providing at least some of the images used for Google Earth (as does DGI), although 67% of its revenue comes from the U.S. government.

OSI Systems (OSIS): Nothing is sacred in the new world order of zero privacy. OSI makes the full-body scanners that scan every inch of your body to find concealed explosives in your underwear.

L-1 Identity Solutions (ID): It knows your fingerprints, can recognize your face via software, can do background checks on you, and will be a big beneficiary of additional military spending and increasing security at airports.

Emergent BioSolutions (EBS) and PharmAthene (PIP): These are the two companies that make vaccines effective against anthrax, the most serious of the various bioterrorist threats. The U.S. government is committed to a strategic goal of maintaining seventy-five million doses of the vaccine in its stockpile. Emergent BioSolutions has an older vaccine that has been around since the 1940s and has all the requisite approvals. PharmAthene should soon have approval for its vaccine. Additionally, it is ahead of competitors in the race to develop a second-generation vaccine. The government wants two suppliers in case one supplier is unable to meet demand during a critical attack.

When it comes to cyberterrorism, investment opportunities are pretty straightforward: virtually all of the companies that connect your company to the outside world are the beneficiaries of increased IT spending to prevent cyberterrorism—in particular, Cisco, which builds the routers that ultimately take your corporate data onto the Internet, and VMware (VMW), which is being increasingly used by corporations to shield their private data and network structure from the outside world.

SEVEN

CLOSE ENCOUNTERS WITH THE DEATH STAR

I T FIRST APPEARED ON Richard Kowalski's computer screen late on the night of October 5, 2008, a tiny pinpoint of light moving rapidly across the field of stars that shone against the black sky. Kowalski, an astronomer working with the University of Arizona, knew instantly what the moving dot meant: he had discovered yet another near Earth object (NEO), one of millions of rocks varying in size from mere inches to miles across that orbit the sun in paths that bring them, by astronomical standards, close to Earth's orbit.

Kowalski quickly forwarded the dot's coordinates to the Minor Planet Center at the Harvard-Smithsonian Center for Astrophysics, which runs a computer program to calculate the orbits of reported objects. Remarkably, the computer failed to analyze the orbit because it was changing so rapidly. When the center's director examined the data a few hours later it appeared that the newly discovered asteroid was being drawn in by the Earth's gravitational field. That suspicion was confirmed soon after by NASA's Near-Earth Object Program Office at the Jet Propulsion Laboratory in Pasadena, Calif.

"For the first time ever, I saw an impact probability of 100% pop up on the computer screen," Dr. Steven Chesley, a scientist at the JPL, later told the *New York Times*. "And this was, needless to say, the kind of thing that makes you sit up straight in the chair."

Scientists estimate the size of the asteroids they discover by the light the objects reflect. This new asteroid, named 2008 TC3, was small, perhaps the size of a Volkswagen, and weighed around eighty tons. They knew that if it really was on a collision course with Earth it would probably disintegrate high in the atmosphere, producing a spectacular fireball but little if any damage.

Over the next several hours, alerted through a global astronomy network, dozens of observatories trained their instruments on 2008 TC3 and began reporting their observations so the Jet Propulsion Laboratory could calculate and refine the asteroid's trajectory. The calculations showed that the object would enter the Earth's atmosphere over the Nubian Desert in northern Sudan at approximately one hour before sunrise. The asteroid disappeared about an hour before that predicted impact as it hurtled into the Earth's shadow and no longer reflected sunlight. But almost to the second a brilliant fireball lit up the sky above the desert. The pilot of a KLM flight some five hundred miles away from the point of impact, alerted where and when to look, saw the flash. Initial estimates that the asteroid had vaporized in the atmosphere proved wrong. An expedition to the Sudan later found about ten pounds of fragments from the asteroid and presented one of those fragments to Richard Kowalski.

In and of itself, Asteroid 2008 TC3 was no big deal. Dozens or even hundreds like it blossom in Earth's atmosphere every year. What made it important is that it was the first extraterrestrial object that had been seen and tracked as it headed for Earth. The fact that human beings were able to do that holds important implications for thinking about the ultimate apocalyptic event, a collision between Earth and an asteroid or comet large enough to destroy virtually all life on our planet.

We know, of course, that meteorites and other space objects bombard Earth constantly. Most are small and friction with our thick atmosphere usually burns them up before they reach the ground. But that isn't always the case. The impact from some very large object millions of years ago was so violent that it likely killed off the dinosaurs. A meteorite exploded over Russia in 1917 with devastating force. Fortunately it struck a mostly uninhabited forest, but it laid waste to hundreds of square miles of trees. There are even theories that the moon was created billions of years ago when an object the size of a small planet smashed into Earth, flinging vast amount of material into space where it coalesced into our shining satellite.

Now many astronomers are tracking the asteroid Apophis, which will pass close to Earth on the inauspicious date of Friday, April 13, 2029. The question is whether the close encounter with Earth will alter the asteroid's orbit enough that it becomes set on a course that intersects Earth's orbit in 2036. In any event, it is worth knowing that astronomers are worried about this problem and have even created a scale to rate potential collisions, ranging from zero for NEOs with no potential to hit the earth to ten for objects that are certain to hit and are large enough to end civilization as we know it. The good news is that nothing we know about now ranks higher than one on that scale and we will probably know something is coming long before it strikes Earth. The bigger that object is the earlier we will know it is coming. The bad news is that we don't know what to do about it. Several schemes for deflecting such a deadly bullet have been proposed, but nothing has been done to prepare. Obviously a category-ten impact would have no investable implications. We would be one with the dinosaurs. But predicted hits by smaller objects and efforts to deflect them are another matter altogether.

Consequences of Collisions

What happens when we collide with an asteroid or comet is all about energy. Objects, even very tiny objects, moving at speeds of 35,000 to 110,000 miles an hour contain tremendous amounts of energy. When they collide with something, some or all of that energy is transferred to the object of the collision. The vast majority of extraterrestrial objects that rain down on us every day simply evaporate in the upper atmosphere, the result of friction between the object and air molecules. It's when the objects are large enough to survive the plunge through the thickening atmosphere that problems begin to arise. They create a searing fireball that can ignite structures or vegetation miles away and throw up immense amounts of debris on impact, which then fall back to Earth and trigger massive earthquakes that can destroy entire cities.

While asteroids and comets are made of different materials and thus carry and dissipate different amounts of energy, astrophysicists begin to worry about impacts with objects that are ninety feet wide or larger. An object that size most likely will explode in the lower atmosphere with a force equal to that of a small atomic bomb. The blast effect that reaches the surface of the Earth may create a crater, would do extensive damage to frame structures, and would result in deaths if it struck above a populated area. As the size of the impactor scales up, so does the damage it does. An asteroid three hundred feet wide—the size of a football field—likely would make it all the way to the surface of the earth and explode with a force larger than any thermonuclear device ever detonated. Should it strike near a populated area the results would be catastrophic, potentially killing hundreds of thousands of people. We can take some consolation in the statistical probability that it would instead slam into the ocean since water covers about 70% of the planet. It might create a tsunami that could affect coastlines surrounding the impact site, but the dynamics of tsunami creation by asteroids aren't well understood.

At nine hundred feet wide an impacting asteroid deals the Earth a mighty blow, creating a crater more than three miles across and laying waste to an area the size of New York (that's the state, not the city!). That kind of devastation would take a huge toll in lives as well as on human psychology and economic activity. Reconstruction efforts would take years and cost billions of dollars.

But it is when the size of the impactor reaches one kilometer—six-tenths of a mile or the equivalent of ten football fields—that the entire planet will feel the effects. Localized destruction would cover thousands of square miles and many millions would die. Governments would topple under the strain and the global economy would edge toward collapse. It would take years simply to recover enough from the shock, both physically and psychologically, to begin any large-scale reconstruction efforts. Perhaps most worrisome, though, would be the potential atmospheric effects that could plunge the planet into the astrophysical equivalent of the "nuclear winter" that would result from an all-out nuclear war. Certainly our current fears about global warming would disappear!

At three kilometers—nearly two miles—wide, all bets are

off. The majority of the world's human population, as well as most animals and plants, would die in the impact or shortly thereafter. Those who survived would then be confronted with the grim outlook of finding enough food, water, and shelter to live in a fashion closely paralleling the lives of cavemen. Truly the apocalypse would have arrived.

Warning: Asteroid Approaching!

The question, of course, is how likely are any of those scenarios to occur? The answer, fortunately, is not very. As the size of the potential impactor rises, the chances that a collision may occur fall. It's simply a matter of numbers. Of the millions of asteroids and comets, most are too small to cause any problems for Earth. And of all those millions of objects, a very tiny number are near Earth objects (NEOs). Further, only a minuscule number of NEOs are in orbits that could result in a collision. Astronomers studying NEOs put the chances of a ninety-foot-wide object striking Earth in the next *century* at 40% and of a football-field sized object at 1%.

The numbers become even more reassuring when we begin to think about objects one kilometer or more in size. That's mostly because the global astronomy community has been searching for those objects for more than a decade. Astronomers calculate that there are probably one thousand or so NEOs that are one kilometer or larger and, as of the last count, they've found and plotted the orbits of the majority of them. Of course, one of the projected asteroids that hasn't been found yet could be on a collision course, but that risk is negligible although not nonexistent.

Rather than focusing solely on these large NEOs, astronomers are beginning now to turn their attention to smaller asteroids that pose a danger to Earth. There are many more asteroids of that size, and they are much more difficult to detect. Their small size reflects much less sunlight than their one-kilometer-wide big brothers and thus more powerful telescopes and imaging systems are required to capture the tiny dot as it moves across the night sky relative to the far distant stars.

Hovering over all of this search activity is the nagging question: What do we do if we find one on a collision course with Earth? As our opening example of 2008 TC3 suggests, there isn't much we can do with the smaller asteroids because they will be much closer to the collision point when we find them. Fortunately, there isn't much we need to do since their impact will produce negligible, if any, consequences.

For the next ten to twenty years, until astronomers have found and done the orbital calculations on asteroids ranging in size from ninety to nine hundred feet, our biggest risk is that we collide with something of that size. We may have some warning or we may have none. The warning, if we have it, will not be far enough in advance to do anything but prepare for the shock, perhaps by evacuating populations most at risk and trying to coordinate global relief efforts. It will be a scary few days.

But what if one of those as-yet-undiscovered large asteroids turns out to be on a collision course? What then?

First, take a deep breath and relax. We will almost certainly have found it many years, even decades, before it meets us at that fateful intersection in the sky. Still, astronomers have been much more diligent about finding these asteroids than governments, our own included, have been about preparing a contingency plan to deal with the problem. The truth is governments are very bad about planning for low-probability, high-consequence events (think 9/11). But when the wake-up call comes, when low-probability becomes certainty, we can be sure that there will be much frantic activity. Unlike the depiction of governments moving secretly to deflect an incoming comet in the movie *Deep Impact* by building a huge spaceship in orbit around the Earth, the news of the impending collision will get out in a matter of hours as astronomers around the world train their telescopes on the asteroid and calculate and recalculate its orbit.

If governments haven't been preparing for the possibility of an asteroid on a collision course with Earth, that hasn't stopped the astrophysicists from thinking about solutions to the problem. While using nuclear weapons to pulverize the asteroid is the popular solution in movies and cartoons, it probably would be a last resort. A more likely and much more effective solution will be to slow the asteroid's speed by slamming an unmanned vehicle onto the surface. A more sophisticated approach would land a rocket on the asteroid's surface that will then use its propulsive power to gently nudge the asteroid off its collision course. Unmanned spacecraft have already orbited and even landed on asteroids, so the technology exists. And it doesn't take much to accomplish the solution given the long lead times involved. Merely accelerating or slowing the asteroid by one mile an hour could deflect its path by about 175,000 miles over twenty years, an ample margin of safety.

The good news is that it is becoming increasingly unlikely that we will one day be surprised by an asteroid or comet big enough to have apocalyptic effects. The chance will never go to zero simply because there are "dead" comets orbiting the sun that don't throw off the characteristic tail that allows their easy observation. They are large, difficult to detect, and moving extremely fast. And we further know that we have the fundamental technology that will allow us to rendezvous with and deflect an object off its collision course. But we still face the possibility that one day the alarm will sound and we will be confronted with having to take the steps to prepare either for a big, albeit not fatal, knock a few days in the future or to organize the necessary long-term defense to save our planet.

Investment Implications of the Death Star

We admit it. It isn't easy to think about investing on the day astronomers announce that they have discovered an asteroid that will collide with Earth. Depending on the size of the asteroid a collision could be the ultimate catastrophe, the kind of event that leaps to mind whenever someone mentions "the end of the world." The problem is the warning time. The collision won't happen suddenly and unexpectedly, taking us all by surprise and leaving us just a few seconds to wonder what that huge flash is all about before we and everyone else are obliterated. We almost certainly will know years in advance if a body large enough to destroy the planet or even inflict immense damage is on its way. About the best we can do is to assume that like people given a diagnosis of a terminal disease, the world will go through the five stages of dying: denial, anger, bargaining, depression, and acceptance.

Denial would be everyone's fondest hope. Maybe the astronomers calculated the trajectory wrong and as they refine their predictions they will discover that it's just a close call, not a direct hit. And that is a distinct possibility. In the anger stage people will demand that someone do something about the damned asteroid. But who will do that? Right now the United States clearly has the best space technology, but will that still be true if the asteroid is discovered twenty years from now and won't hit for another thirty years after that? Japan, Russia, China, and India are all getting into the latest round of the space race and could develop superior technologies in the next few decades. More to the point, though, who makes the decision about what should be done? Governments around the world cannot even decide jointly what to do about climate change, which has known solutions. Coordinating a highly technical and expensive effort to nudge an asteroid into a new orbit will be well beyond their capabilities. That's when the bargaining starts: Which nations will put up how much money and what kind of technology? How will we pick the person to lead the effort? Who has veto power over the various proposals that will arise? Which companies will do the work? How in the world do you make money in that kind of environment?

Principle One: Fade the Fear

Every time there have been rumors of a NEO that could potentially hit the Earth, they have either turned out to be false because the data was misread in some way or because when it was finally reanalyzed, it turned out that the NEO was not in fact on a collision course with the Earth. This is the stuff by which media events are created. An asteroid potentially hitting the Earth will force you to not switch channels until you get the full story. You might even click on a website or two. Page views are created, advertisers are happy, publishers are happier, you become satisfied that you can sleep easy at night ("Phew! No asteroid will hit today") and all is well again in the world.

But for that brief moment in time, there was panic, albeit momentary. We don't realistically think that an asteroid will hit the earth (it's one of those high-consequence events that has such a low probability it's almost not worth thinking about). That said, this is the purest example of what this book is about—a hype-driven, media-driven "world-ending disaster," which will affect the stock market for an entire news cycle—until it subsides. We might as well make money on it while we can.

And should an asteroid be on a collision course, well, it's

nice to know that governments are finally starting to examine how to divert that asteroid. We will focus on these efforts for our Principles Two and Three.

But first and foremost, if the market were to drop even one penny because of fear of an asteroid hitting (and again, this is a metaphor for any media-driven fear that has an infinitesimally small chance of actually occurring), you must fade that fear. Buy the market. Buy the stocks that are most brutally hit because of the fear. The market will return once the news cycle is over—just like it does every day when we have "micro media asteroids" hitting all day long.

Further to this point, James has even studied the phenomenon of "market asteroids." He examined all the stocks in the S&P 500 to find those occasions when a stock fell more than 20% in a single month. When a stock loses value this quickly, it usually means some disaster really did happen: maybe the company missed on earnings expectations, the CEO was charged with a crime and resigned, or the company's accounting was revealed to be entirely fake? Were investors right to panic?

There have been 2,919 occurrences of an S&P 500 stock falling 20% in a month during the past twenty years. On 1,645 occasions (57%), the stock was higher six months later. On average across all 2,919 occurrences, the stock was higher an average of 10.5% during that time period, significantly higher than the average return of 2% on the S&P 500 during similar six-month periods. In other words, investors who see an asteroid in the sky immediately conclude that it will hit and destroy the company. But it seldom happens. The asteroid swings past on its orbital path and then disappears into space. The lesson? In general, when a stock falls 20% in a month, buy the stock.

Principle Two: Invest through the Back Door

If astronomers ever determine that in the year, say, 2043, an asteroid is going to come close enough to Earth that we need to start investing in technologies to deflect it, then it's important to invest in some of the major aerospace companies. These companies will put together massive proposals to send out rockets to blow up or divert the asteroids, and billions will end up being spent. This most likely will be for nothing, but we might as well benefit. Since this is such an unlikely event, the idea of using the "back door" is that we should only invest in the companies that will continue to grow even if no asteroid hits.

Lockheed-Martin (LMT) is a great example. The company (as of this writing) has raised its dividend six years in a row, through good times and bad. They make rockets, airplanes, navigation systems, missiles, etc.—all the things you need to run a good air war, send satellites into space, or deflect an asteroid.

Raytheon (RTN) is a competitor to Lockheed-Martin, and its earnings also grew through the recent recession. If a company can both deflect an asteroid and grow earnings during a financial crisis, then it's a perfect back-door play.

Northrop Grumman (NOC) is also in the aerospace and defense industry and also has consistently raised its dividend for seven straight years, including through the recent recession.

Principle Three: Invest through the Front Door

There are specific companies that specialize in the technologies that will be necessary to successfully intercept and deflect an asteroid. Much will depend on the specific plans for pulling off this technological Hail Mary pass, but two companies that would be logical candidates to participate are Orbit International (ORBT) and Orbital Sciences (ORB), both of which have strong ties to the military.

These companies provide many of the nuts and bolts technologies used in the aerospace and defense industries for creating small- and medium-class rockets and the technologies on those rockets. Other companies in the space industry include Ducommun (DCO), which makes everything from switches to specific metals that are used on the rockets to the various electromechanical components that help special-purpose aircraft or rockets accomplish their tasks. The company was formed in 1949 and has consistently grown earnings through recessions, wars, and good times.

A chapter about asteroids almost seems flippant in a book that discusses real Earth-threatening disasters that we face on a daily basis. The serious threat of another terrorist attack, or the eventual pandemic that will plague the earth, or even the billions being spent on environmental issues, are all threats that our society must deal with, spend money on, and face their eventuality. But it's important to note that even the lowest-probability events could affect the markets, even for those brief moments when the news cycle hits them with a fury. Being ready for those events and using the principles described above as an investment reflex will help you ride out the worries and prosper.

EIGHT

GAME OVER!

The End of Capitalism

ALMOST EVERY TIME THE stock market has fallen signifi-cantly over the past one hundred years it's because people think that, at long last, the great experiment we call capitalism has failed. What's eerie about this scenario is that even if capital-ism fails, the world will still be standing. But for people who own homes, stocks, or any assets, it will feel like the end of the world. In 1929 the Great Depression led many to wonder if capitalism was on its last legs. Then in World War II fascism became a pal-pable threat to our financial way of life. More recently the dot-com bust and then the much more severe Great Financial Collapse of 2008 looked as if they would pull capitalism down.

We can certainly paint a realistic scenario of a global finan-cial collapse. Many banks could fail, and the rest of the world would lose faith in the U.S. dollar. Our only source of new money would be to simply print it, and the value of the dollar would plummet. ATM machines would stop working as failing banks were no longer able to process transactions in real time (the FDIC would take over the processing so they could guarantee printing enough money to satisfy demand). Unemployment would skyrocket as companies failed to obtain the necessary credit lines to meet payrolls. Homes would be lost and once wealthy families could succumb quickly to poverty.

In 2008 we came close to this kind of financial apocalypse, and there's been a lot of discussion about what caused the financial crisis of 2008–9 and what the ultimate consequences of the crash truly are. There's also the question: can it happen again? And what happens if the financial system is allowed to collapse? If governments refused or were unable to structure bailouts of massive financial firms, what would be the consequences? To understand how to invest in "the end of capitalism" we need to look at these issues:

- What caused the crisis? Recognizing the symptoms could potentially lead to a future diagnosis that would allow us to avoid a similar crisis.

- What actually happened in the crisis? What was the chain of events that led to the collapse of Lehman, AIG, and potentially the entire banking system? This is different than looking at the fundamental causes because it asks the basic question: was it really a crisis at all?

- How did it happen that the global banking system reached the verge of collapse in only a few days?

- What would have happened if the banking system would've been allowed to collapse? Hank Paulson, the secretary of the Treasury, when arguing for the $700 billion bailout in September 2008, warned Congress that if "we don't pass this bill we may not have an economy by Monday." Was that really true? And finally, can we get back to our basic principles in the middle of a financial crisis so that we can make some money?

One thing that was clear during this financial crisis is that 99% of the trading and investing strategies that were bread and butter to thousands of hedge funds, mutual funds, and traders all fell apart.

What caused the crisis? Everything you've read before is wrong.

The Financial Crisis of 2008–9: A Case Study

There have been countless books, articles, pundits, economists, and bloggers commenting on the "Great Panic of 2008," but most, if not all of them, miss something. They primarily focus on the most immediate cause of the crisis: in the years prior to the crisis banks reduced lending standards and made more loans than they should have to people who were not creditworthy. When you loan money at high interest rates to people who are not creditworthy, bad stuff happens. People default. Homes are lost. But this was not the reason for the financial collapse. At the time of the collapse, relatively few people had yet foreclosed, hardly any banks had failed, and unemployment was still sitting around 5%.

Superficially, what happened was that many institutions, ranging from hedge funds to traders to banks, both foreign and domestic, shared in the risk of these loans through derivatives called mortgage-backed securities (MBS). Mortgage-backed securities were pools of potentially thousands of loans. The idea was that if any one loan defaults it was not such a big deal because all of the other loans were paying. If the pool of loans, on average, was paying a 7% mortgage, then the buyer of the MBS could expect at least a 5% yield, no problem, even if there were quite a few defaults. If the buyer of the MBS could buy the security using leverage (i.e., borrowing at 3% to buy the MBS at 5%), then the ultimate yield to the buyer is even greater. This assumes, of course, that the level of defaults does not exceed what was modeled by the buyer or by the buyer's lender, or by the buyer's lender's lender. So there was lending on top of lending on top of lending.

But this has all been in the newspapers. We know that hedge funds and banks borrowed to buy securities that already had a highly leveraged component and so on. There was an enormous amount of leverage, but that still wasn't the basic cause of the financial collapse either, although it was probably the last straw on the poor camel's back.

Let's rewind a bit and peel back the decades past the glory

years of the 1990s, when money seemed to be growing on trees, back through the stagflationary 1970s, the swinging 1960s, and the innocent conformist 1950s. The ultimate cause of the financial crisis in 2008–9 was World War II. The "greatest generation" was sick and tired of the Depression. Their sons, fathers, brothers, and friends had died for their country, and those who came home or who had stayed home wanted their rewards.

What happened in World War II? We know all the usual history: Pearl Harbor, the atomic bomb, the Axis powers, etc. But the most important part for this chapter was this critical issue: sixteen million men left the workforce and just as many women rose to take their places. When the war ended and the men came back, women continued to stay in the workforce. The "two-income family" became a reality and, of course, two incomes mean more money to spend.

The Great Depression had cast a pall over everything and that pall lasted until 1945. Nobody wanted to spend during a war so it took the end of the war, the beginnings of the baby boom, and the entry of sixteen million women into the labor force to really get the new party started. It's a party that kept going for decades.

We got used to our cushy new suburban white-picket fence lifestyle in the 1950s and began to enjoy not just two incomes, but also rising net worths as the stock market boomed in the 1960s. But our hunger to spend became increasingly insatiable, and we became a nation of consumers. Madison Avenue was in full swing, hawking washing machines, sugared drinks, shiny cars, and exciting lifestyles never experienced before.

How could we get even more? Enter the 1970s when inflation took over. Inflation is not necessarily a bad thing. When the value of the assets we own increases (as is initially the case in inflation), we feel like spending more because our net worth has increased. It's only when the things we want to buy start to get a lot more expensive that we suddenly realize, "Oh no! Something is going horribly wrong here!" And although stagflation tempered our desire to spend temporarily in the mid-1970s, we regained our confidence just in time for the reign of Ronald Reagan.

The spending craze that began in 1945 with the beginnings of dual income families had to continue. Fortunately, the leveraged buyout boom of the 1980s fed that need. Billions of dollars were pumped into the system via the leveraged buyouts engineered by Michael Milken and others. The stock market roared as a result, again increasing the net worth of the average American household, allowing us to spend even more. And this continued into the 1990s with the dot-com boom and the IPO boom.

The dot-com bust, which led to a severe plunge in the stock market, left us with one final asset class that we could use to finance continued spending: our homes. The Federal Reserve had cut interest rates to almost 0%, causing mortgage rates ultimately to plummet, allowing people to buy houses affordably, at least initially. But what started rationally turned into massive speculation in housing, causing housing prices to escalate sharply. In the ten-year period between 1997 and 2006, housing prices increased a whopping 124%. In some areas of the country the increase was much greater.

Consumers used this increase in the value of their homes, combined with the looser lending standards of the banks that regulators permitted, to withdraw cash from their houses in the form of loans so they could continue their spending. Cash withdrawn from houses for spending totaled $627 billion in 2001 but increased to $1.4 trillion by 2005. American home mortgage debt increased from an average of 48% of GDP in the 1990s to 73% of GDP in 2008. This was fueled by the increase in securitization by the banks, by Fannie Mae and Freddie Mac, and by hedge funds and other non-bank lenders. The more institutions securitized our debt and sold them off, the more they could lend out again. This wasn't a bad thing. It made us feel more flush. Until it was abused.

The housing speculation was a big part of the collapse, but not all of it. The other issue was that we were spending so much on foreign goods that the trade deficit ballooned. This caused foreign governments to flood our financial system with dollars, allowing risk to be spread around across asset classes (because banks and lenders knew, or thought they knew, that they could always share the risk on assets with foreign investors), which allowed banks to lower lending standards.

So here's what happened: A bank would lend John Smith $1 million to buy a house. The bank would then "service" that loan and collect the monthly payments. But the bank would not take on the risk. It would package that loan as a "mortgage-backed security," bundling it with thousands of other loans so any one loan would no longer matter. Hedge funds would in turn borrow money (from other banks) to buy up bundles of these mortgage-backed securities. Risk would be spread so widely it would seem as if there was no risk at all. Which made it easy for insurance companies to insure against the risk of default on these securities. But once defaults started to go from 1% of the mortgages to 2%, then 3% and then 4%, the massive amounts of borrowing used to bundle, package, and buy these securities began to unravel. A country with "only" a ten-trillion-dollar GDP like the United States couldn't handle the cascading defaults.

The housing bust officially began in 2007 but it took until early 2008 before the effects were fully felt in the financial industry. In one weekend, Bear Stearns collapsed and was "bailed out," beginning the chain of government intervention that attempted to prop things up. Bear Stearns was ultimately sold to J.P. Morgan in a government-brokered intervention under the guise of "the whole financial world would've collapsed if we didn't do this." In September 2008, with Lehman Brothers on the verge of collapse, the government decided, "You know what? We're going to let this little baby collapse and see what happens." Sadly, that was the wrong decision. The collapse of Lehman Brothers almost led to the collapse of AIG, the massive insurance company.

AIG had been allowing institutions like Goldman Sachs and Morgan Stanley—other banks that were lending to Lehman—to insure against the collapse of Lehman Brothers with hundreds of billions of dollars worth of credit default swaps. Now

AIG was faced with having to pay those claims. The insurance giant couldn't afford it. The collapse of AIG would have led to the collapse of every bank that had lent to Lehman and had insured against the default of those loans. Additionally, all the people insured by AIG would no longer have insurance.

Once Lehman collapsed, money market funds got into trouble. Many money market funds lent to Lehman in the form of "commercial paper." When individuals need small, short-term loans, they usually borrow off of their credit cards. When big, supposedly safe companies need small short-term loans they borrow from banks in the form of commercial paper, essentially loans that usually roll over within a day or so. The money used to fund these small loans comes from the money market funds where many of us park our extra cash. Here's the problem: when Lehman collapsed, it defaulted on its commercial paper, causing money market funds to "break the buck," i.e., trade for less than the money investors had put into them. This had never happened before. So people panicked and took their money out of the allegedly "safe" money market funds, leaving little to finance the issuance of commercial paper. Worse, the banks did not want to lend to one another because they feared a borrower might collapse and the U.S. government wouldn't move to save it.

Lending froze. Nobody was able to borrow any money, even the safest of companies. Had the government not intervened at that point it is conceivable that the lending freeze would have persisted and led to the collapse of a major bank like Citigroup. Nobody would have been able to take money out of their bank accounts. Companies would not have been able to meet payroll. A scenario far worse than the Great Depression could have resulted.

Imagine going to an ATM machine for Citigroup or Bank of America—whatever your bank is—and nothing comes out of the cash dispenser. You try another ATM. Still nothing. You check your balance and the ATM machine says, "Error. Please try later." Imagine your boss trying to make payroll by doing his usual trick of financing his receivables for a week or so until the checks arrive. Except now not only can he not do that financing (no banks will lend) but the checks never arrive. The dollar would weaken to nothing as foreign governments would be unable to lend us any more money. The currency would collapse.

Was this possible in those fateful days after Lehman collapsed? Maybe this is extreme. But without intervention certainly all of the major banks could have collapsed, including Citigroup and perhaps Wells Fargo and Bank of America. Approximately $30 trillion in reserves would have been taken out of the system just when we most needed it to buy food, gas, or diapers for our kids.

We'll never know for sure what would've happened. And despite hundreds of books and articles that will eventually be written about the crisis, nobody will be able to say for sure which steps we took were correct and which were wrong or overdone.

Is it a fait accompli that the economic boom that followed World War II will ultimately sputter out and create a subsequent period of worldwide financial havoc? While we don't know for sure, we do know that the government's stimulus has a basic feature that can take us back to our frontier roots.

The key is not how much money can we borrow and then print. Rather, the question is whether the money the government spent on stimulus will actually stimulate businesses, increase lending, and ultimately create greater income for individuals and tax receipts for the U.S. government. The bet is that, yes, banks will start to lend again, companies will get started or will grow off as a result of the new lending, more employees will be hired by these growing companies, and these new employees will suddenly need new houses, new cars, and new TVs. And a weakening dollar will make our goods more attractive to foreign customers, invigorate domestic manufacturing and industrialization, and increase local tax revenues allowing us to pay back our debts.

Will spending return to what it once was? We'll see. As of now, the U.S. savings rate is the biggest it's been in years. People are literally stuffing cash in their pillowcases because they are afraid of more bank collapses, more financial crises, zero interest rates, and another Great Depression. This is not really a good thing for the country as a whole, and it illustrates the "savings paradox." When times are good, we want people to be able to save their new money so they are ready for hard times. But when times are bad, we desperately need people to stop hoarding their money and spend as much as possible.

The following graph comes courtesy of the St. Louis Federal Reserve:

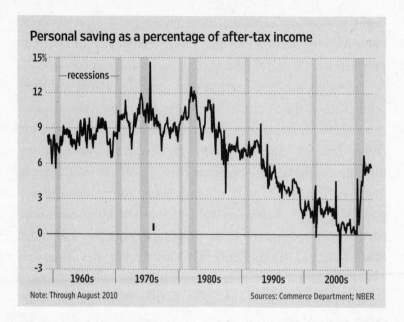

Personal saving as a percentage of after-tax income

recessions

15%
12
9
6
3
0
-3

1960s   1970s   1980s   1990s   2000s

Note: Through August 2010   Sources: Commerce Department; NBER

It isn't a coincidence that the savings rate spiked in the midst of the Great Financial Collapse. People are afraid to spend money and the result is that businesses aren't growing, unemployment is high, and the nation is mired in what certainly feels like a recession. However, there is a direct connection between a higher savings rate and future consumer spending. With this in mind it's good to expect the best, but prepare for the worst.

Let's get back to the basic principles. Most of the time when the market is worried about the end of the world, it really doesn't end. Whether it's a recession, a financial crisis or a banking panic, eventually the world recovers. But that doesn't mean you can blindly buy the dips. Financial companies (banks, insurance companies, nonbank lenders, investment banks, and consumer finance companies) have been permanently altered by the financial crisis.

Investment Implications of a Financial Collapse

A financial collapse is almost always preceded by a bubble of massive proportions. The housing and Internet bubbles and busts demonstrate this well. After the bubble bursts, many books are written about what caused the bubble, what could've prevented the bubble, what could've prevented the crisis that resulted, and what could be done to fix the system so that such a bubble never occurs again.

The first thing is, there's nothing wrong with a good bubble every once in a while. We know this is almost religious blasphemy. Many people are horrified at the sheer greed and speculation that takes place in a bubble.

But in order to fully appreciate the financial advice we will give in this chapter, you need to realize that bubbles are a part of life and often result in great innovation and progress for society. Go ahead right now, look at yourself in the mirror, and say, "Bubbles are OK. I'm going to make money in the next bubble."

Why are bubbles OK?

Massive wealth is created. Venture capitalists raise money and invest it in young entrepreneurs. Companies go public or get acquired. Much wealth is destroyed during the inevitable bust that occurs, but rarely enough to take us back to levels of national net worth that existed prior to the bubble.

Important innovation occurs. Without the Internet bubble, as an example, nobody would've created Google (the twentieth search engine out there when it was started, it was funded by angel investors who made money on other tech deals). It remains to be seen what innovations will come from the housing bubble, but not every financial innovation that was used to finance housing will turn out to be "bad." Derivatives will be reformed but they are here to stay now and will eventually be used to finance new innovations in the economy.

As beneficial as these bubbles may be, they will eventually burst, and you should be prepared for that as well. When a financial collapse occurs, several things will happen:

- Interest rates will drop.

- Stimulus money will be spent, much of it on public works.

- Balance sheets will get cleaned up. (Enron's and World-Com's disappeared in 2002, and in 2009 all the bank balance sheets got cleaned up to a great extent.)

Let's focus for a moment on the stimulus money injected into the economy by the government, since that's what will enable us to make money out of a financial collapse. While this money may or may not help the financial companies, what we know from previous experience in busts is that the one thing that will benefit from stimulus spending is the nation's highways. "Let's fix our highways!" is the rallying cry of the Keynesian economists ready to jolt the economy back into action. When the economy starts to recover, we'll usually see these changes begin to happen, and investors should keep them in mind:

- Companies benefiting from the stimulus will hire more employees, causing the unemployment rate to go down.

- New employees combined with reduced inventories from homebuilders, combined with temporarily lowered interest rates thanks to the Fed, will create new demand for housing—demand that will be sustained by actual growth instead of poorly conceived lending standing standards.

- A new economic boom will begin—a boom that will outlast the post–World War II boom because it will be based on a more sound financial system which learned the lessons from the recent collapse.

Principle One: Fade the Fear

One way to "fade the fear" in a financial crisis is to buy companies that have dipped but will still benefit from the financial stimulus that will inevitably occur. (Note: we're not referring to any specific financial stimulus. Every financial crisis will be followed with a financial stimulus as governments scramble to avoid perceived disaster, whether incorrectly or correctly.) A few good examples include Astec Industries (ASTE), which supplies the asphalt used in highway repair, Lindsay Corporation (LNN), which provides the project management for highway and bridge repairs, or Nucor Steel (NUE), which supplies the steel used in bridge construction projects. Furthermore, a large part of the latest stimulus package included modernizing the nation's electricity grid, so companies such as MasTec, which improves communications and utility infrastructure, should benefit.

Principle Two: Invest through the Back Door

In this case, the back door is that whenever a financial crisis occurs (since the 1600s), reform follows. The back door is investing in the companies that benefit from this reform.

After the banking panic of 1907, the Federal Reserve was created. After the 1929 collapse, the Securities and Exchange Commission was created. Even after the 1987 crash, reforms were put in place to shut the market down if it fell too quickly in the course of a day (the so-called "circuit breakers").

One aspect of our current financial system that will invariably need reforming is the increasing use of derivatives. As makes sense, a derivative is a security that is *derived* from another security. A security might be a stock in a company, say IBM. That stock might be trading for $120. You might want to buy the right to buy IBM for $140 anytime within the next year. If you own that right (called an option), even if IBM hits $180 within the next year, you still have the right to buy it for $140. That option is a derivative because it's a separate security, but its price is derived from the price of IBM stock.

As reforms in derivative trading are considered, one group of companies will surely benefit over the next decade. These are the exchanges: the New York Stock Exchange (which trades under the symbol NYX), the Nasdaq (NDAQ), the CME (CME), and the Intercontinental Exchange (ICE).

Currently, banks trade derivatives privately, in a shadow system. Reforms in derivative trading are likely to change that. Just as I can't buy and sell IBM stock privately with my neighbors (by law, securities must be traded through an exchange), I wouldn't be able to buy and sell highly complicated, esoteric derivatives. The steep increase in secretive derivative trading played a big part in the financial collapse of 2008–9, a full year after housing prices had started to slip. Bringing these derivatives into the light means bringing them into the exchanges.

It would be nice and easy if stimulus and reform saved the day as outlined above. And having highway and materials companies in your portfolio as well as the stocks of the various exchanges are good, diversified ways of playing the outcomes of any financial crisis. It's also a good strategy for creating a broadly diversified portfolio in less dire economic circumstances.

But, that said, let's also prepare for the worst.

Principle Three: Invest through the Front Door

Here are some investment principles that will directly benefit the investor in case of a collapse.

Borrow against any hard assets you own. This may seem contradictory, given that borrowing could cause a financial collapse. However, there are two scenarios that could occur if you borrow as much as possible against your house:

- *We have a hyperinflation environment.* No problem, you took your borrowed cash and put it into commodities that went up in value. It will be easier for you to pay back your loan and have a profit on top of it.

- *We are in a depression and a deflationary environment.* No problem, the value of your house has gone way down—much faster than gold and silver, which *still* might go up even if your house goes down—and you may have lost your job, but thankfully you pulled valuable cash out of your house while you still could. As a result, you are able to feed your family and wait out the difficult times.

Invest in companies that benefit from depressions. While many companies will obviously struggle, several categories of companies benefit during a financial crisis.

- Pawnshops—companies such as Cash America (CSH), or First Cash Financial (FCFS), are chains of pawnshops. Pawnshops go up in a crisis for several reasons. First, the banks have shut out nontraditional borrowers who were feeding off of the banks largess immediately before the crisis began. These borrowers, now short on cash to pay their debts to the traditional banks, will have to pawn assets to survive. Second, those assets—in some cases gold and other jewelry—will go up in value due to the stimulus creating an inflationary environment.

- Software companies that benefit from increased mortgage and foreclosure activity—companies such as Lender Processing Services (LPS), which provides the banks with software to help process foreclosures, is an example of a company that directly benefits during a crisis.

- Debt collectors—companies such as Portfolio Recovery Associates (PRAA) or Asset Acceptance (AACC) buy portfolios of consumer debt that the big banks have written off. The banks are happy to get it off their books so they sell the portfolios of bad debt for pennies on the dollar. Once the economy begins to recover, the debt collectors will begin collecting at a higher rate than the banks thought they would've been able to collect.

Avoid shorting the market. When the markets are going down in what seems like a straight line (as they were in October 2008, September 2001, and even December 2000), it's not a good idea to short. Nothing moves in a straight line and whenever the market moves down quickly, volatility starts to spike higher. Surprisingly, higher volatility is not a friend of the determined short seller. To illustrate this, let's look at the top ten up days in the Nasdaq's history.

DATE	RETURN
1/3/01	14.17%
11/13/08	11.81%
12/5/00	10.48%
10/28/08	9.53%
4/5/01	8.92%
4/18/01	8.12%
5/30/00	7.94%
10/13/00	7.87%
10/19/00	7.79%
5/8/02	7.78%

Note that all ten of the highest up days in the Nasdaq's history occurred during bear markets. Imagine if you were to not only short the Nasdaq, but short the Nasdaq's most volatile stocks during the thirty days of December 4, 2000, to January 4, 2001. You probably would've been wiped out as a short seller. And this was during the worst bear market the Nasdaq had ever experienced. Many of the Nasdaq 100 stocks fell 99% during the period from 2000 to 2002, and yet short sellers were in serious danger of getting wiped out on the many up moves that were experienced during this period.

So an important rule during a financial crisis, or any earth-shattering crisis, really (and this is advice we repeat throughout and cannot stress enough): do not short sell.

Instead, follow the recommendations above in our basic principles: find the companies that will benefit from infrastructure development and stimulus, find the companies that will benefit from increased reform, and look for companies that benefit from the alternative banking environment that results because of a financial crisis.

Will a financial collapse occur again? It's always a possibility. Learning to recognize the signs (the potential collapse of financial institutions, the negative personal savings rate we briefly experienced, a feeling of irrational boom, etc.) combined with learning how to protect yourself and your family could help you ride out the worst of times. We are not over the current financial crisis and won't be for years.

In any world-shaking crisis you want to rely on your own wits first and never be dependent on the foresight and generosity of others. In a financial collapse, the world might be going down around you but you are less likely to succumb if you keep track of your own assets and have as much control as possible.

CONCLUSION

A COLLISION WITH AN ASTEROID is one of our apocalyptic scenarios, and we sincerely hope it never occurs. But the fact is we confront unknown threats to ourselves and our markets constantly. They're like lots of tiny asteroids bombarding us. As we write this, for example, the tensions between North Korea and South Korea are threatening to erupt into warfare and possibly pit the United States against China once again. This first half of 2010 was, globally, the hottest on record, with places like Moscow sweltering under an unprecedented heat wave that killed thousands of people. Pakistan has suffered monumental flooding that could further destabilize its already shaky government. Another oil rig has exploded in the Gulf of Mexico and a violent earthquake has shaken New Zealand.

All of these concerns are fueled by media outlets that are deeply addicted to creating fear. If nothing was going wrong anywhere, what would all the reporters, anchors, and bloggers have to say? But of course bad things happen all the time, and markets fluctuate as a result. "Asteroids" appear on the horizon and some investors and traders panic. What if the asteroid hits? What if that major customer is lost and never comes back? What if that restatement of earnings means the company is a fraud? What if the CEO selling shares means he knows something we don't?

Sure, there are lots of reasons to worry, but we know from past experience that justifiable worries can quickly turn into unjustifiable panic—and vice versa. Investors aren't the rational beings that economists make them out to be, and, just as they act on unjustified fears, they can also become irrationally optimistic. When that happens we get a bubble. Investors saw this with tech stocks in the late 1990s, houses in the early 2000s, and tulips way back in the 1600s. Most people in the market when the bubble bursts will panic and sell, driving prices way below their fair value. That's when you want to be buying all those stocks everyone else is dumping.

Amid all the worries that constantly plague us, though, it's important to keep these disasters in perspective. Where there is a real possibility of a pandemic, we also need to keep in mind that giant pharmaceutical firms like GlaxoSmithKline and much smaller specialized companies like BioCryst Pharmaceuticals are working on both preventive measures and cures. And just as there is a long-term threat that the world will run out of fresh water, we need to remind ourselves that global behemoths like General Electric and small players like Energy Recovery are working on ways to convert the plentiful supply of salt water into fresh water we can drink. The capital and creativity behind these efforts to solve looming problems should give us a sense of confidence that mankind can meet the challenges it faces. More to the point of this book, that confidence will show itself over the years in the form of rising prices for the stocks of such innovative companies.

Especially after crises, it's easy to feel like victims, with terrible things happening to us because of Mother Nature, terrorists, financial markets, or bad luck. The ethic of this book is that we don't have to accept the role of victims in the face of catastrophe. Like anything else, we want to fight back, recover, and prosper. Our financial lives are no different. If we have the knowledge and fortitude to think about investing in this way and the intellectual curiosity to look beyond the superficial, then we can profit by investing in the apocalypse.

In a collapse, and even prior to one, always remember the three principles discussed in this book:

Principle One: Fade the Fear. Stocks will fall, as described in the example of the "market asteroids" above, and that often produces the best time to buy.

Principle Two: Invest through the Back Door. Choose growing, consistent companies that demonstrate success—in both good times and bad—and that happen to have divisions or products that will grow to meet the demands caused by the crisis.

Principle Three: Invest through the Front Door. Pick stocks whose entire purpose is to deal with the demands caused by the crisis.

Our strategy needn't become the entire focus of your portfolio. Only you can determine what role it will play given your own time frame, assets, and goals. But keep in mind how long mankind has walked the earth and what we as a species have accomplished. It's a great story and justifies in every way our first principle: Fade the Fear!

A QUICK GUIDE TO APOCALYPTIC INVESTING

PANDEMIC	WHAT TO LOOK FOR	WHAT TO DO
FADE THE FEAR	The initial outbreaks that trigger fear of a pandemic.	Whatever markets are falling on the initial fears, buy. Example: Hong Kong in the 2004 SARS fear.
BACK-DOOR INVESTING	Big pharmaceuticals that have divisions working on vaccines.	Possible examples are GlaxoSmithKline (GSK), Pfizer (PFE), etc.
FRONT-DOOR INVESTING	Companies focused on developing specific vaccines.	Example: BioCryst Pharmaceuticals (BCRX) working on drugs to prevent viral infections.

DIRTY WATER	WHAT TO LOOK FOR	WHAT TO DO
FADE THE FEAR		
BACK-DOOR INVESTING	Conglomerates with water treatment businesses.	Buy General Electric (GE) and Jacobs Engineering (JEC).
FRONT-DOOR INVESTING	Companies specifically focused on aspects of the water treatment industry.	Examples: Idex Corp. (IEX), Mueller Water Products (MWA), Insituform (INSU).

PEAK OIL	WHAT TO LOOK FOR	WHAT TO DO
FADE THE FEAR	An oil spill, or an extreme weather event that triggers global fears on lack of supply of oil.	Buy the major oil companies (XOM, CVX, etc.), or buy consistent dividend payers (MCD as an example).
BACK-DOOR INVESTING	Large companies that have a growing (but still small) division focused on alternative energy.	Example: Archer-Daniels Midland (ADM), a company that produces corn, among other things, but also has a division for ethanol.
FRONT-DOOR INVESTING	Companies that make it easier to drill for hard-to-find oil.	Examples: Diamond Offshore (DO), Transocean (RIG).

GLOBAL WARMING	WHAT TO LOOK FOR	WHAT TO DO
FADE THE FEAR		
BACK-DOOR INVESTING	Companies in mainstream industries that have alternative fuels as a byproduct.	Example: Otter Tail (OTTR), a utility company that has a division focused on wind power.
FRONT-DOOR INVESTING	Companies whose sole focus is alternative energy.	Example: Cameco (CCJ), the world's largest uranium producer.

TERRORISM	WHAT TO LOOK FOR	WHAT TO DO
FADE THE FEAR	Stocks crash on initial attacks or fears of attacks.	Gradually buy the broad-based market (SPY).
BACK-DOOR INVESTING	Solid conglomerates that have divisions for defense.	Buy companies such as General Electric (GE), Lockheed Martin (LMT), or Tyco (TYC).
FRONT-DOOR INVESTING	Companies that specifically target identifying or preventing terrorist attacks.	Example companies include VeriSign (VRSN), NICE Systems (NICE), and OSI Systems (OSIS). Other examples are in the chapter.

A Quick Guide to Apocalyptic Investing

FINANCIAL COLLAPSE	WHAT TO LOOK FOR	WHAT TO DO
FADE THE FEAR		
BACK-DOOR INVESTING	Financial crisis reform.	Invest in financial exchanges.
FRONT-DOOR INVESTING	Government spending on public works.	Invest in stocks like: Astec Industries (ASTE), Lindsay Corporation (LNN), Nucor Steel (NUE).

JAMES ALTUCHER'S APOCALYPTIC READING LIST

While I like to think we have provided the complete reference on the end of the world I realize that there might be other references out there that would help increase your understanding of the different issues that confront us. Knowledge is the ultimate weapon, and with that in mind here is my recommended reading list.

Dread: How Fear and Fantasy have Fueled Epidemics from the Black Death to the Avian Flu by Philip Alcabes
  Explores not only the history of pandemics since the Black Death but also discusses how even the word "epidemic" is often overused in order to illicit fear in the populace. An excellent discussion that would leave one prepared the next time some potentially devastating infectious disease begins to rear its ugly head.

A Guide to the End of the World: Everything You Never Wanted to Know by Bill McGuire
Discusses issues ranging from asteroid collisions to overpopulation.

SuperFreakonomics by Steven Levitt and Stephen Dubner
In addition to being a thoroughly interesting book on a range of topics, the book contains an excellent counterview in the global warming debate.

The recent financial collapse of 2008 is worth a list all by itself. Here are some of the books we recommend reading to understand the deeper reasons behind the collapse and whether or not it can happen again. Some of the books are from before the collapse but are still considered required reading:

Against the Gods: The Remarkable Story of Risk by Peter Bernstein
When the stock market is on fire (somewhat rare in the past decade but it will occur again) the concept of risk gets thrown out the window by most investors. Peter Bernstein's book is a reminder that risk is there in every asset class and will bite you if you are not aware of it.

The Greatest Trade Ever by Gregory Zuckerman
An amazing blow-by-blow account of how John Paulson and a few others made the greatest contrarian investment ever and stuck with it long enough to make billions.

The Road from Ruin: How to Revive Capitalism and Put America Back on Top by Matthew Bishop
This book brings up the point that in every bubble, the financial innova-

tions that caused that bubble were eventually put to good use by the economy, and that we can't ignore the financial innovations that may have caused this bubble (rampant securitization and derivatives).

Power Hungry by Robert Bryce

Another look at climate change and alternative energy.

The Next 100 Years by George Friedman

Friedman is the founder of Stratfor.com, a news website that seems to have its hooks in various intelligence agencies around the world in order to provide the latest up-to-date analysis of what is happening during crisis events. The book gives his theories about the major trends effecting the next century and in particular gives his reasons why the twenty-first century will be called the American century.

The Black Swan by Nassim Taleb

Taleb takes the view that often betting on the completely unexpected is the way to make the most amount of money. Unfortunately, due to this book, and perhaps due to its timing just before the great financial collapse, everyone is now betting on the next Black Swan. The contrarian bet now seems to be to bet that things slow down, volatility goes down, and the market simply continues its one-hundred-year journey to new highs.

The Real History of the End of the World by Sharan Newman

A great reminder that the concept of predicting the apocalypse is so prevalent in our world history it's most likely a product of our DNA. The author documents three thousand years' worth of end-of-the-world predictions and shows the countless times people were waiting for, well, nothing.

Crisis Economics: A Crash Course in the Future of Finance by Nouriel Roubini

"Dr. Doom" himself, Roubini is credited for predicting the hard landing on the U.S. housing market as early as late 2006 before prices really began to break. That said, he also predicted the end of the economic world several times in the previous five years.

It's Getting Better All the Time: 100 Greatest Trends of the Last 100 Years by Julian Simon

A counterpoint to the end-of-the-world theorists. Written in 2001 by the late Julian Simon, the economist demonstrates one hundred trends that have shown significant improvement over the past one hundred years.

The Rational Optimist: How Prosperity Evolves by Matt Ridley

Perhaps the best modern (written in 2010) sequel to the above book, countering many of the doom-and-gloom theories that are currently out there.

The Forever Portfolio by James Altucher

While it seems shameless to promote the book of one of the authors, *The Forever Portfolio* discusses long-term trends ranging from increasing obesity to terrorism to health-care issues, which makes it a good companion to this book.

INDEX

Note: Page numbers in *italics* refer to charts and graphs.

Index

Index

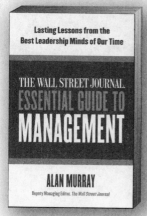

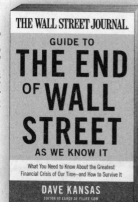

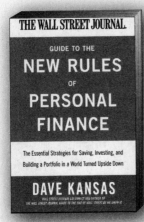

THE WALL STREET JOURNAL GUIDE TO THE NEW RULES OF PERSONAL FINANCE

Essential Strategies for Saving, Investing, and Building a Portfolio in a World Turned Upside Down

By Dave Kansas

ISBN 978-0-06-198632-1 (paperback)

In this definitive guide to the new world of personal finance, Dave Kansas takes everything you thought you knew about saving, managing risk, and constructing a portfolio and turns it upside down. Incorporating old ideas that still work with new strategies and tactics, this book will help investors take advantage of the radically new financial world.

THE WALL STREET JOURNAL GUIDE TO INVESTING IN THE APOCALYPSE

Make Money by Seeing Opportunity Where Others See Peril

By James Altucher & Douglas R. Sease

ISBN 978-0-06-200132-0 (paperback)

This essential guide advises savvy investors on how to anticipate and prepare for seemingly earth-shattering events—how to measure the risks and adjust their investments—to gain a substantial advantage in reaping profits while others are frozen with fear.